Po...

JOINT STANDING Committee
for THE Pottery Industry

DEPARTMENT OF EMPLOYMENT

Pattern for Progress

Second Report of the Joint Standing Committee for the Pottery Industry

738·19

LONDON: HER MAJESTY'S STATIONERY OFFICE 1971

SBN 11 360885 3

Foreword

From 1918 there has been almost constant consultation between manufacturers, employees and HM Factory Inspectorate, initially through the National Joint Council of the Pottery Industry up to 1945 and then from 1956 through the Joint Standing Committee set up as an advisory body to HM Chief Inspector of Factories. In 1960 the Committee, including representatives from the British Ceramic Research Association as well as the British Pottery Manufacturers' Federation, the Ceramic and Allied Trades Union* and HM Factory Inspectorate was established as a statutory body by the Minister of Labour to

"keep under review and to advise him from time to time on matters affecting the health, safety and welfare of persons employed in the pottery industry".

so continuing the tradition of co-operation and consultation. The First Report of the Committee 'Dust Control in Potteries' was published in 1963.

Since that time the Committee as periodically re-appointed has continued to meet twice a year but much of the technical work has been channelled through the Technical Sub-Committee (up to 1967 the Potters' Shops Sub-Committee) which has met more frequently and has included co-opted members from the B Ceram. RA.

This report of the work of the Committee departs from previous practice in that rather than merely recording action taken it attempts to present a comprehensive view of the present state of the industry and to indicate possible future trends affecting health and safety. Furthermore the report is addressed directly to those engaged in the industry and with its more attractive presentation will, it is hoped, give positive guidance to all who are concerned with these aspects of this important industry. A report such as this must inevitably look back, and in the pottery industry there is much to regret, but real progress can now be recorded and the future can be faced with optimism.

In the case of pneumoconiosis the delay between exposure and diagnosis is such that the benefits of earlier recommendations by the JSC will not yet be fully revealed, but they should become increasingly apparent in the next decade.

Although the sections of the report have been integrated, each may be separately considered as complete in itself. It is hoped the report will provide a pattern for progress not only in the pottery industry of Great Britain but that it will also prove helpful to other industries or countries where similar health problems have yet to be solved.

* Known as the National Society of Pottery Workers up to 1 1 70

Members of the Joint Standing Committee

J A Davis (Chairman)
HM Superintending Inspector of Factories Midlands (Nottingham) Division.

BRITISH POTTERY MANUFACTURERS FEDERATION

J M W Davis   E James Johnson
A G Ellis   N Richards
R Fletcher   N L Wright

CERAMIC & ALLIED TRADES UNION

J K W Arnold   A Martin
A Dulson   L R Sillitoe
S Dutton   N Walters

BRITISH CERAMIC RESEARCH ASSOCIATION

A Dinsdale

HM FACTORY INSPECTORATE

J D G Hammer HM District Inspector of   D J Evans (Secretary)
Factories, Stoke-on-Trent

PREVIOUS MEMBERS

Chairmen

Miss K Crundwell (1956-59)
Miss M Brand (1959-63)
E Waller (1963-67)
Miss L A Pittom (1967-70)

**British Pottery Manufacturers
Federation**

R J Bailey (1963-69)
Lt. Col. C G M Boote (1964-69)
E R G Corn (1956-64)
R J M Howson (1964-69)
R Basil Johnson (1956-64)
A J Lewis (1956-64)
D P Shelley (1959-68)
N Wilson (1956-63)

Ceramic & Allied Trades Union

J E Clowes (1957-63)
H Hewitt (1956-65)
S Hobson (1956-66)
L Jackson (1956-65)
W Tranter (1956-64)

H M Factory Inspectorate

G P Brown (1963-67)
V B Jones (1959-62)
Miss L A Pittom (1962-63)
W G Symons (1956-59)

Secretaries

N Fish (1956-62)
P H Royle (1962-66)

Mr S H Jerrett, Director, and Mr D Turner, Secretary of the British Pottery
Manufacturers Federation attended meetings as observers.

Contents

Safety
by Design

Safety principles are clarified and applied to materials and methods used in production in order to indicate ways of minimising the risks of injury and ill health. Progress over past decades is acknowledged and present developments considered in the light of the stated safety principles, with emphasis on the need for continuing co-operation from all sides of the industry.

It is suggested that improvements in both productivity and safety could result from the integration of safety principles with technical change.

Safety Parameters

If all danger from the operation of plant, from the use of materials or from the working environment were eliminated, the result would be absolute safety in that there would be no hazard additional to those normally encountered in everyday life. Whilst this must be regarded as the ideal it is virtually impossible to achieve because some danger can arise even in the best regulated industrial environment. In practice, therefore, the aim must be to reduce the hazard, whether it be a mechancial hazard from plant, or a health hazard arising from materials, to insignificant proportions, thus achieving intrinsic safety. Where this standard cannot be attained measures to control the latent hazard must be superimposed. Since, however, such measures require monitoring to ensure their continuing efficacy, the primary aim should always be to make the plant or material intrinsically safe.

Applying these principles to the elimination of mechanical hazards, it must be conceded that few machines can be rendered absolutely safe, but intrinsic safety may be achieved by so positioning the dangerous parts within the machine so that they are inaccessible to the machine operator and to other workers during normal operations at the machine. Where it is not possible to eliminate the danger to the worker in this way then the hazard must be controlled by providing a protective guard or establishing a permit to work system. Such control measures must, of course, be constantly maintained and Part 2 of this report demonstrates in part, failures in this respect. At the same time there are now encouraging signs that some machinery manufacturers are giving more attention to safety at the drawing board stage.

Applying these same principles to the elimination of hazards to health, intrinsic safety involves the identification of hazardous materials and their substitution by safer ones. This technique is as applicable to those new developments which could introduce new dangers as to the well known and long standing problems of free silica* and lead. The use of siliceous bodies for pottery manufacture over the centuries has established practices which are not easily abandoned, but encouraging progress is now being made in the search for body formulations having a lower free silica content[1,2]. Although the total free silica in the body gives a convenient indication of hazard potential from a single analysis, a better index of hazard would be the proportion of free silica in the respirable[3] size range.† As the proportion of free silica in the respirable dust is generally lower than that in the body the convenience of assessing the potential hazard by the body composition introduces an additional margin of safety.

The free silica is either introduced as a constituent of the basic ingredient, principally clay and stone, or separately added as flint or sand. Any progress towards intrinsic safety is most likely to result from the development of substitutes for these separate additions of free silica but benefit would also flow from any increase in particle size of ground material containing free silica as this would reduce the proportion of free silica in the respirable dust.

While materials containing a substantial amount of free silica continue in use, a wide range of dust control techniques is essential. Although hazard control of this sort might hitherto have been regarded as the normal approach, the latent danger to health may in fact be more effectively eliminated by modifying the process to achieve operational safety. In this context operational safety demands the substitution of dust-free production methods for those which generate respirable dust so as to ensure that the latent hazard of the material cannot present any risk to the workers.

The past emphasis upon hazard control has required first the suppression of dust or the provision of means for its control at specific dust-producing operations, namely, the primary dust sources. Although this has mainly involved the development of captor hoods for specific processes or machines where the primary dust is evolved, complete separation of the hazard from the worker's environment might be achieved by containing the production processes entirely within a closed system[4]. Secondly, however, hazard control must take account of the miscellaneous or secondary dust sources which result largely from the handling of ware and the escape of bulk material from the production system which subsequently gives rise to atmospheric dust[5,6,7]. While the control of primary dust sources can be achieved by the application of exhaust ventilation to existing machines or systems of production, greater difficulties have to be overcome and even manufacturing techniques changed if secondary dust sources are to be entirely suppressed. In either case, the standard of control required to be achieved depends upon the degree of risk as indicated by the hazard potential. Because in some sections of the industry this remains high, it is

---

* Silica is the dioxide of silicon (SiO_2) which is said to be free when not chemically combined into other compounds.

† Respirable dust means the particles of such size that they can penetrate to the Alveoli of the lungs.

particularly encouraging to note instances where changes in manufacturing processes have resulted in operational safety, such as the substitution of wet sponging for dry towing[8], but beyond this, the closer the approach to intrinsic safety, the less strenuous need be the effort to achieve operational safety and hence the lower the cost of implementing the appropriate level of safeguard. At a time when the law of diminishing return is seen to be operating in the steeply rising capital and operating costs of each successive step of hazard control, the cost-mitigating influence of intrinsic safety could be of great benefit.

The addition of safeguards to an existing production system involves not only high initial expenditure but also significant continuing costs of operation and maintenance. As in the design of machines which are intrinsically safe from a mechanical point of view, the costs of safeguards to health can be minimised by integrated safety planning, first by eliminating the hazards as far as possible at source and then by incorporating precautions against those which remain, whether arising from plant, process, working situation or material, as an integral part of the plant or production system.

Review of Progress

Progress towards intrinsic safety has not been restricted to a reduction in the soluble lead content of glaze or the substitution of non-hazardous materials for china biscuit placing and polishing. Other hazardous materials have been largely eliminated and the introduction of potential new hazards averted by the vigilance of the Committee[1]. Nevertheless, despite the continuing search for new materials, in practice the principle of intrinsic safety has not yet been achieved in body compositions but rather have dust control methods been added to previously existing conditions.

At the time of the First Report* and following the specific requirements of the 1950 Regulations (SI 65 1950) primary dust sources were the main concern of the industry and control methods devised by the B Ceram. R A were recommended. These recommendations, based on the knowledge of the time have been generally followed but they related to the then current conditions and needs, and consequently may be less applicable to more recent developments.

Efforts to extend control techniques to other known sources of primary dust have continued and in some

instances have been linked with a re-appraisal of production methods[9]. one electro porcelain fettling hood was based on the abandonment of the traditional 5 ft board for ware carrying, improved methods of scrap control are being applied at various fettling hoods and the progressive change from dry towing to wet sponging of flatware[10] will eliminate a hazardous operation. Individual manufacturers no longer content to leave the initiative to collective effort have actively sought the incorporation of high standards of dust control on new plant rather than accepting its subsequent design and addition at a later stage.

As the control of primary dust sources improves, so secondary dust sources increase in importance particularly where the rate of production rises. Although the emphasis of the First Report recommendations was placed upon primary dust sources which gave high dust concentrations in the vicinity of the operator, consideration was also given to some secondary sources which resulted in general pollution of the workroom atmosphere. The principle source of secondary dust considered in the First Report was overalls and the advice then given has been fairly well observed but there has been need for following up that advice. (Joint Standing Committee for the Pottery Industry, 1967c). It must be stated, however, that the recommended non-absorbent fabric is often unpopular especially where workroom temperatures are liable to fluctuation.

Although specially selected to minimise dust retention and re-evolution, terylene fabrics still release dust when soiled with clay.

In 1968 and 1969 a worker was diagnosed as a pneumoconiotic as a result of mainly post-war exposure to dust rising from pottery overalls in laundries (Evans & Posner, 1971). The design of overalls has developed only slightly, boiler suits being tried in one factory, while a sanitary ware manufacturer has converted the recommended trousers to 'Bermuda' shorts. The earlier recommendations, despite the accompanying invitation to modify the basic design, have been regarded as rigidly specific so deterring desirable developments. Provided that the principles of fabric selection on grounds of minimal dust evolution and a design based on minimum dust pockets are observed, there could be a flexibility in applying the recommendations to particular situations. Means of preventing possible build up of dust on overalls by more frequent laundering or de-dusting would be desirable.

Dust evolution when handling flatware at some automatic towing machines was partly controlled by modifying the extraction hood provided to control primary dust.[11],[12] Little progress has yet been made at

* Dust Control in Potteries — First Report of the Joint Standing Committee for the Pottery Industry (Ministry of Labour, 1963).

other secondary sources although advice on the control of scrap, possibly the greatest cause of atmospheric dust, can now be given,[13] The transfer of some of the worker's responsibility for cleaning his own area to a separate force of cleaners has encouraged a neglect of good housekeeping which is so essential to minimise secondary dust sources. Generally, safety has not been neglected in the pre-occupation with health matters. The continuing upward trend of accidents has indicated the need for investigation in order that remedies may be devised. The value of a wider approach to particular problems has been demonstrated in the case of kiln accidents and also the recent enquiry into handling accidents.[14]

The conversion to natural gas, well advanced in North Staffs, is not thought to give grounds for special concern, providing the advice previously given on safety in the use of towns gas is carefully followed, but the recent thorough investigation of safety in the use of natural gas made by the Committee under the Chairmanship of Prof. Morton (Ministry of Technology, 1970) is welcomed. Whatever fuel is used, it is essential that safe procedures be laid down and carefully followed and when making conversion to natural gas it should not be assumed that the previous safeguards are still appropriate and the advice of the Industrial Gas Engineers of the local Gas Board should be followed.

In the potteries, as in industry generally, safety has been regarded as an addendum to a process or plant which has been designed primarily to meet the requirements of production and some developments have actually introduced additional problems. The unsatisfactory standards achieved, often at substantial cost, by attempting to graft safeguards on to unsafe processes or plant has encouraged the development of a more comprehensive approach to safety planning.

Current Developments

The recent increase in willingness to incorporate safety into the basic production design is welcomed. The voluntary co-operation of machinery manufacturers, potential machine users and HM Factory Inspectorate has improved the standard of safeguards against injury through accidents or to health at many new machines. It is hoped that this trend will be further encouraged by HM Chief Inspector giving guidance as to when satisfactory standards have been reached, so enabling users of new machinery to assess plant on grounds of safety as well as of efficiency.

Mechanisation is continuing at an increasing rate,[15] particularly where mergers have facilitated rationalisation and increased scale of production, and where new capital has been made available. As new machinery is introduced there is increasing responsibility upon management to see that it is satisfactory in every respect before it is brought into use and that this standard of safety is maintained.

In order to meet the need for training personnel to deal with wider and more complex safety problems, the Works Inspectors training courses have not only continued but have now been expanded to include some general safety training. The same trend is illustrated by the introduction at the North Staffs Polytechnic of a general safety training course for graduates and management in the ceramic industry.

The effectiveness of the Works Inspectors scheme is sometimes in doubt even where restricted to the duties as defined in the Regulations. Too often the Works Inspector's work is cursory and his reports ignored, a situation which in time discourages further effort. The responsibility for such a situation of report-without-remedy rests with the management. The real function of the Works Inspector should be to monitor conditions and so enable management to take prompt action to remedy any defects. Where the person appointed has been delegated sufficient authority to secure remedies on behalf of management, or where reports of deficiencies are energetically followed up the scheme makes a useful contribution to safety and health.

The group inspection system has been developed in recognition of the need for monitoring by an Inspector with training and skill, and with sufficient time and detachment from production pressure. Some companies with several factories or individual factories, by subscription to a group scheme, can now secure the service of such an Inspector, but the effectiveness of any scheme still depends upon the implementation of the advice given.

Mechanisation of existing processes no longer consists of mechanical simulation of skilled operations but often includes an appraisal of production methods and associated developments. This is well illustrated by the present generation of machines to eliminate towing, long recognised as a hazard.[16] New clay shaping methods with better moulds have virtually eliminated the need for face towing of flatware and edges can be satisfactorily smoothed with a wet sponge as with cast hollow-ware. This related development has enabled recent mechanisation to utilise wet edge sponging as a substitute for dry smoothing operations. Mechanisation without careful consideration of its effects on dust generation could increase difficulties as in the mining industry from which in 1935 it was suggested that pneumoconiosis had 'quietly vanished' (Hunter, 1955). However, by 1955 the problem had re-emerged with even greater force and this was attributed to the extensive mechanisation of coal-getting methods.

Greater efforts are also being directed towards silica reduction and intrinsic safety. Co-operative research is being undertaken by the B Ceram. R A and the suppliers of materials to the industry, as well as by individual pottery manufacturers. Although this research has not led to any general change in practice, there is an encouraging development in the use of lower silica bodies in hotelware manufacturing. Whereas much of this research has been stimulated in the past by the general continuing investigations into body formulations for the purpose of production which might also benefit health, some manufacturers are now motivated by the desire to reduce the silica content of the body and ultimately to achieve intrinsic safety in order to benefit the health of the workers.

Workers are also being encouraged to safeguard their own health, especially by the proper use of overalls and high standards of housekeeping, so minimising secondary dust. Failure by operatives to conduct their work to the maximum advantage may sometimes be the result of inadequate training or supervision. The Industrial Training Board now ensures that safety and health are included in all approved training schemes and the workers' contribution to the safety of his environment has been emphasised in the Newsletter of the Ceramic and Allied Trades Union and by posters specially prepared for the industry.

HM Factory Inspectorate has also shared in the continuing work of training at all levels, from operatives through meetings with the union, to a half-day seminar with senior directors in 1969.

The Way Ahead

Recent developments in ceramic technology and the structure of the industry have engendered a willingness to relinquish the ties of tradition. This attitude to change, as well as the changes themselves, can now be exploited to secure improvements in safety and health.

Further changes in body composition as already facilitated or necessitated by the availability of raw materials and developments in manufacturing techniques are likely to result from the continuing research into methods of production and materials used. Exploitation of these changes as at present foreshadowed by the introduction of reduced silica hotelware body may well lead to an extension of low silica body recipes so resulting in a greater measure of intrinsic safety. Nevertheless, this is a long term project and there will be a continuing need for production methods to be designed to operate safely.

The control of primary dust sources at mechanised operations has enabled some stages in production to be totally enclosed. The future need will be the integration of these separate units into a comprehensive flow line system based on the principle of closed circuit production. Modern tile making plant and large capacity domestic ware production units are already developing in this direction. Such standards of enclosure which would ensure complete control of both primary and secondary dust sources are unlikely to be generally attainable in the more immediate future, particularly in the small and less mechanised factories. Here, remedial action will still be required to deal separately with these categories of dust sources especially in those processes which the present health survey[17] may reveal as potentially more hazardous.

Means of controlling the major primary dust sources are now available and future emphasis should be placed upon the elimination or control of secondary dust, especially that arising from spillage and floor cleaning. Again, these precautions are best incorporated at the planning stage. Likewise, general safety will also require careful consideration in the planning stage in order that danger can be averted or precautions incorporated.

Thus the need for the future will be integrated safety planning and total environmental engineering, to which end research and development should be directed. There will be an ever greater need for close co-operation between plant and pottery manufacturers, workers and HM Factory Inspectorate to ensure that changes are not only manipulated but also motivated to secure maximum improvement in working conditions. Thus by the application of integrated planning future developments should lead to improvement in both productivity and general conditions of work in the pottery industry.

1, 5, 8, 10, 11, 16   Part 3 Domestic Whiteware Manufacturing
2, 6   Part 3 Sanitary Whiteware Manufacturing
3   Part 4 Dust Measuring
4, 7   Part 3 Tile Manufacturing
9   Part 4 Dust Control
12   Appendix 4.1 Semi-automatic Towing Machines
13   Part 4 Scrap Control
14   Part 2 Accidents
15   Part 2 Structure of the Industry
17   Part 2 Dust Disease

Indications
of Progress

Pneumoconiosis and accident
records over a period of 20 years
are considered against the
background of variation in the
numbers employed in the North
Staffordshire pottery industry.

An upward trend in the number of
accidents is indicated and data
analysed to determine some of the
causes and to suggest remedies.
Pneumoconiosis figures do not
lend themselves to similar analysis
as they depend on the age and
experience structure of the working
population which has not been
established. Nevertheless, grounds
are found for optimism and
encouragement to continue efforts
to minimise exposure to dust.

Structure of the Industry

In 1956 a census of employment in the North Staffs pottery industry was undertaken as part of the Industrial Health Survey. (Ministry of Labour and National Service, 1959). Similar, but not identical censuses were completed in 1959 and biennially thereafter by HM Factory Inspectorate in Stoke-on-Trent for the Joint Standing Committee. In 1956 and 1969 only, enquiries were broadened to cover, in outline, all British potteries. Further particulars of this series of censuses are to be published. (Gregory and Smyth, in preparation).

The overall employment figures, summarised in table 1, reveal a general reduction in the number of workers of 20% during the period 1956 to 1969, but this contraction was by no means evenly spread over each class of product within the industrial divisions of the pottery industry. In contrast with this general contraction is the slight rise in numbers employed in wall tile manufacturing (shown as Tiles — earthenware), industrial fireclay production and in the separate pottery service industry undertaking milling and glaze and colour production.

The changing size of the pottery labour force has also been accompanied by changes in distribution between sexes, adults and young persons, and full and part time female workers as indicated in table 2. The reduction in male adult workers was only 9% while the reduction in the total number of full-time female adult workers was 31%. The number of female adult workers employed for less than 30 hours and therefore categorised as part-time has increased by almost 50% from just under 1,580 in 1956 to almost 2,400 in 1969.

The number of young persons employed in the pottery industry has diminished by 43% since 1956, again with a greater reduction in the number of female young workers than male. The number of school leavers entering the pottery industry as operatives has shown a very marked reduction, falling from over 900 in 1958 to just under 400 in 1968 but rising in 1969 to over 460. (City of Stoke-on-Trent, 1958-1969.) Little is so far known of the age structure of the workers in the pottery industry and of the relationship between the number of years service in the industry and age. Attempts are now being made to obtain this information to facilitate a better understanding of the pneumoconiosis statistics. Manpower statistics prepared by the Department of Employment and Productivity (West Midlands Region) in 1968 revealed that 11% of the pottery workers were over 55 years of age and about the same proportion under 21 years. In the year mid-1967 to mid-1968 it was

Table 1. Number of workers in North Staffs potteries by product/body classification

| | Thousands | | | | | | |
	1956	1959	1961	1963	1965	1967	1969
Sanitary							
Fireclay	.6	.6	.5	.5	.5	.5	.5
Vitreous china*	1.7	1.4	1.4	1.4	1.4	1.2	1.3
Total	2.4	2.0	1.9	1.9	2.0	1.7	1.8
Domestic							
Earthenware	22.2	20.6	19.6	19.8	18.9	18.4	17.7
Bone China	6.7	6.7	6.1	5.6	5.2	5.3	5.7
Mixed	4.5	4.5	4.5	3.5	3.6	3.9	4.2
Decorating	.6	.4	.7	.6	.6	.5	.4
Total	34.1	32.2	30.9	29.5	28.3	28.2	28.0
Tiles							
Fireclay	3.3	2.5	2.1	1.1	.9	.6	.6
Earthenware	3.3	3.5	3.9	3.9	4.0	3.5	3.7
Total	6.6	6.0	6.0	4.9	4.9	4.0	4.3
Industrial							
Fireclay	.2	.5	.5	.4	.4	.7	.7
Vitreous china*	4.1	3.4	3.6	3.3	2.9	2.6	2.2
Total	4.3	3.9	4.0	3.7	3.3	3.2	2.9
Materials							
Mills	.8	.6	.7	.6	.6	.5	.6
Glazes	.02	.3	.3	.4	.4	.5	.6
Total	.8	.9	1.0	1.0	1.0	1.0	1.2
Totals	48.2	45.1	43.9	41.0	39.6	38.1	38.3

* In this and subsequent tables sanitary vitreous china includes earthenware which it has now replaced; and industrial vitreous china includes porcelain as used in electro-ceramics.

Table 2. Composition of the North Staffs pottery labour force 1956-1969

| | Thousands | | | | | | |
	1956	1959	1961	1963	1965	1967	1969
Males 18+	18.03	17.16	16.67	15.80	15.68	15.42	16.44
Females 18+							
Part-time	1.58	1.75	1.58	1.86	2.08	1.92	2.38
Full-time	25.64	23.36	22.92	20.44	19.43	19.03	17.85
Boys	.80	1.00	1.00	1.05	.77	.68	.70
Girls	2.14	1.85	1.75	1.83	1.59	1.03	.97
Total	48.14	45.12	43.92	40.97	39.55	38.08	38.34

Source (tables 1 & 2): Census of Employment in the North Staffs Pottery Industry, HM Factory Inspectorate, Stoke-on-Trent.

Table 3. Distribution of North Staffs pottery workers between basic processes 1956-1969

| | Thousands | | | | | | |
	1956	1959	1961	1963	1965	1967	1969
Milling	.74	.65	.70	.88	.68	.59	.58
Sliphouse and dust preparation	1.01	1.06	1.03	.94	.98	.97	.89
Shaping other than pressing	12.01	10.69	10.51	10.52	10.15	9.64	9.08
Pressing	1.68	1.85	1.74	1.40	1.30	1.02	1.20
Biscuit placing and warehouse	4.24	3.51	3.24	3.00	2.87	2.77	2.81
Glazing and glost warehouse	10.89	9.81	9.66	8.86	8.73	8.17	7.93
Decorating	10.64	10.19	9.55	8.45	7.97	7.61	7.61
Other	6.89	7.35	7.51	6.92	6.88	7.33	8.25
Totals	48.14	45.12	43.92	40.97	39.55	38.08	38.34

Table 4. Pottery factories in North Staffs by product/body classification

| | Thousands | | | | | | |
	1956	1959	1961	1963	1965	1967	1969
Sanitary							
Fireclay	3	3	3	3	3	3	3
Vitreous China	9	6	6	6	6	6	6
Total	12	9	9	9	9	9	9
Domestic							
Earthenware	119	98	100	98	93	87	78
Bone China	47	38	41	36	32	32	34
Mixed	6	6	6	3	3	4	3
Decorating	42	29	36	33	33	30	27
Total	214	171	183	170	161	153	142
Tiles							
Fireclay	25	18	16	11	11	8	9
Earthenware	14	13	10	13	11	11	11
Total	41	31	26	24	22	19	20
Industrial							
Fireclay	5	5	9	8	6	6	6
Vitreous China	12	11	11	12	11	9	7
Total	17	16	20	20	17	15	13
Materials							
Mills	28	28	26	24	22	21	23
Glazes etc.	3	7	13	14	12	12	11
Total	31	35	39	38	34	33	34
Totals	315	262	277	261	243	229	218

estimated that about 11,000 workers were recruited to the industry to compensate for an equivalent number of leavers giving a labour turnover of almost 30%. A more recent investigation (National Board for Prices and Incomes, 1970) has set the labour turnover at 43% for adult male workers and 58% for adult female workers.

The distribution of workers among the basic processes has changed only slightly (table 3); 'Other workers' shown in the table include mould makers, labourers, maintenance men, etc. who now constitute a greater proportion of the total labour force.

While the labour force was declining by 20%, the total number of factories or establishments* in North Staffs engaged in pottery manufacturing dropped from 315 to 218 (table 4), a reduction of 33%. This reduction was especially marked in the domestic and tile section of the industry where the reduction in the number of factories was 33% and 50% respectively. Raw material preparation and glaze production is clearly becoming a more separated service industry. The contracting number of factories does not represent adequately the reduction in numbers of firms* and enterprises*, mergers and take-overs within the pottery industry have led to the emergence of a few large groups especially in domestic and wall tile manufacturing, although all parts of the industry have experienced a measure of consolidation. So far many of these amalgamations have affected administration and marketing organisations rather than changes in operations.

This present trend could further influence the future size of the pottery working population and hence the number of workers likely to be exposed to potentially hazardous conditions. Except in the case of factories classified as manufacturing fireclay tiles and industrial earthenware, which are concerned primarily with the production of fireplace and floor tiles and electrical porcelain respectively, the average factory size has risen. The overall average size has grown from 292 workers per factory in 1956 to 388 in 1969, the largest single increase, from 328 to 388, occurring during the period 1967 to 1969.

* as in the Census of Production (Social and Economic Research Interdepartmental Committee 1969).

Establishment — refers to whole premises under the same ownership or management at a particular address.

Firm — one or more productive establishments operated under the same trading name.

Enterprise — one or more firms under common ownership or control.

Source (tables 3 & 4): Census of Employment in the North Staffs Pottery Industry, HM Factory Inspectorate, Stoke-on-Trent.

The geographical distribution of the British pottery industry (table 5) still reveals a concentration in the North Staffs area, where 68% of all pottery factories are situated and 82% of pottery workers are employed; as most of the raw materials are imported into the area and locally mined coal is no longer used as fuel, the main reason for this continued concentration must surely be tradition, local skills, research, training and available services. However, the proportion of the nation's pottery workers in Stoke-on-Trent has fallen and so has the proportion of factories, although to a lesser extent, on account of the large number of small factories producing general earthenware, particularly the studio type potteries directing their output towards the holiday trade in the southern counties.

During the period of declining labour force and number of factories, the output of most branches of the industry has risen, but not to the same extent as all manufacturing industries (Machin and Smyth, 1970). The rise in output from the different sections of the industry has also varied; domestic production has been restored to the 1948 level as indicated by the index of output corrected to 1948 price (Machin and Smyth, 1970) while the output of glazed tiles has increased by almost 100% in the same period. The census of production covering only larger firms* revealed that nearly half the entire British pottery output came from the 15 enterprises in each of which 1,000 or more workers were

* As in the Census of Production (Social & Economic Research Interdepartmental Committee, 1969). A larger firm is one having on an average more than 25 workers during the year.

Table 5. Distribution of the major divisions of the GB pottery industry 1956 and 1969

Percentage of all GB employees in the divisions employed in North Staffs potteries.

	1956 a	1969 b
	%	%
Sanitary		
Vitreous China	46	35
Fireclay	21	31
Domestic		
Earthenware	94	90
Bone China	91	83
Tiles		
Wall and Floor	77	65
Industrial Earthenware	57	48

Source:
Col. a Industrial Health: (Ministry of Labour and National Service 1959).
Col. b HMFI Stoke-on-Trent.

employed. These enterprises, 10% of the total, included 25% of the establishments and accounted for 44% of the workers.

Material Supply

The tradition that each pottery should be fully self contained was first eroded by the growth of separate colour and glaze manufacturers. In North Staffs the preparation of raw materials has also become largely separated except in the case of the very large potteries.

In 1956, 68 pottery manufacturers in North Staffs, including some relatively small ones, undertook their own milling and glaze preparation, but by 1969 the number had fallen to 35. The number of workers engaged in milling and glaze preparation in these factories fell from 325 in 1956 to 147 in 1969. It is estimated that flint calcining and milling was carried on in 16 different pottery factories in 1956 but by 1969 there were only five. The number of separate mills undertaking this work also fell from 22 to 10 during the same period. The number of flint producing plants has further reduced to a total of 13. Material preparation is now being extended beyond ingredient processing to include preparation of pottery body. Delivery of prepared body, rather than raw ingredients, is likely to grow and may well be combined with the use of spray dryers to enable the dried body to be delivered by tanker and discharged pneumatically into sealed silos for feeding direct to some of the new generation of machines which are now becoming available. Centralised body production, like the contraction of the flint processing industry, could further reduce the number of workers engaged in the more hazardous process of handling dry ingredients with a high silica content. This development, already well advanced in some European countries (Weiland, 1970) holds the promise of a high standard of operational safety by largely closed circuit production and ensures that a really high standard of dust control can be achieved.

Dust Disease

Summaries of pneumoconiosis assessments for pensions attributable to the North Staffs pottery industry prepared annually for the Joint Standing Committee give accumulated detailed information which enables a review to cover a period of 20 years and also facilitates the comparison of totals for two decades. More general information for all British potteries and other industries is also available from the annual reports of the Department of Health and Social Security (DHSS 1944-49, 1950-69). Attempts to draw conclusions as to progress in overcoming the dust hazard is not easy as the data relates only to cases where the victim has made application for compensation and where pneumoconiosis has not only been diagnosed but is sufficiently advanced as to cause disability. Particulars of the schemes under which compensation can be paid is given in appendix 2. Although the trend in assessments (figs. 1 & 2) appears to indicate encouraging progress, the number of new pensions awarded each year give only a very rough guide as to the actual incidence of the disease and certain other critical factors have to be considered, such as the changes in the schemes and the diagnosis of the disease.

Changes in schemes and assessments

The marked rise in the number of assessments noted in the mid 1950s was common to nearly all industries where dust disease occurs, including mining, and similar sharp rises occurred at about the same time in other countries (Gilson, 1969). Changes in the scheme of benefit and in the degree of disablement for which pneumoconiosis pensions were granted (appendix 2) contributed to this rise.

The interruption in the schemes of initial and periodic medical examinations of workers in specified processes set out in appendix V of the First Report (Ministry of Labour, 1963) by the Medical Panels under the Workmen's Compensation Act caused by the preparation of the new arrangements under the 1946 Act, resulted in a backlog of cases which came to light when the scheme became fully operational after 1954. This late discovery would tend to give high average disability in the years immediately following. On the other hand early diagnosis resulting from an almost simultaneous reduction in levels of assessed disability from 5% to 1% at which pensions were granted would tend to lower the average level of disablement on first assessment. Taken together these factors would cause a peak in the annual totals without further significantly changing the average disability. This did not in fact happen in the case of the pottery industry because the discovery of the backlog of cases did not await the full resumption of regular medical examinations (fig 3a) but results from the earlier work of the miniature mass radiography service (see Diagnosis), which covered all workers and not only those in specified processes.

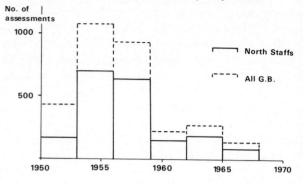

Figure 1. Assessments for pneumoconiosis pensions 1950-1969

All GB and North Staffs potteries 3-yearly totals.

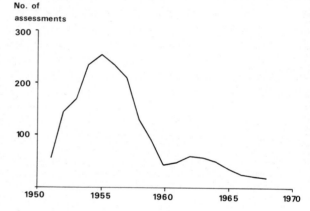

Figure 2. Assessments for pneumoconiosis pensions 1950-1969

North Staffs pottery industry moving average over 3 years.

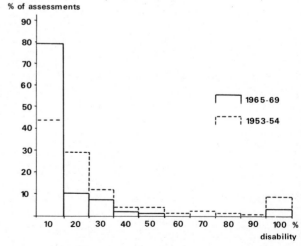

Figure 3a. Assessments for pneumoconiosis pensions in the North Staffs pottery industry. Distribution by disability 1953-54 and 1965-69

The removal of the restriction on compensation to actual loss of earnings by the introduction of recompense for loss of faculty encouraged a large number of applications and further contributed to the rise in the number of pensions awarded. (Department of Health and Social Security, 1940-1949, 1950-1969). The effect of this last change, which was widely publicised, is indicated in the rise from an average of 27 current pensions attributable to the pottery industry before 1954 to an average of 179 over a 5 year period after the change (Appendix 3.1.). Of the 1300 partially disabled workers in all British industries awarded pensions in 1954, the great majority had previously made unsuccessful claims. (Department of Health and Social Security 1950-1969).

The cumulative influence of all these factors would be expected to cause a sharp rise in assessments in the years immediately following the changes, and subsequently a fairly swift reduction to a new equilibrium level.

Diagnosis

With the changes in the schemes of compensation and the level of award, there was a rising awareness of the disease as the result of which more workers demonstrated their readiness to be X-rayed (Ministry of Power, 1955). This readiness coincided with the development of the miniature mass X-ray service and surveys carried out at collieries and other dusty workplaces, especially where there was a concentration of a particular industry as in the case of pottery and cotton manufacturing.

The local unit of the miniature mass radiography service was established in Stoke-on-Trent in July 1952, under its present director Dr. E Posner and the mobile unit was used to carry out the first survey in the pottery industry between 1952 and 1954. Including the cases of category 1 simple pneumoconiosis, which would not normally result in pensionable disability, the number of cases detected rose from 200 in the first year to over 400 in each of the two following years. Further surveys in the pottery industry were carried out in 1955-58, 1959-62, 1963-66 (Birmingham Regional Hospital Board, 1953-1970. Posner 1969). The effect of the first diagnostic survey was quickly reflected in the number of assessments by the Stoke-on-Trent Pneumoconiosis Medical Panel. In 1953 the number rose from an average of 55 for the years 1950-52, to an average of 221 for the next six years, after which the total fell sharply to about the pre-1953 level, and has since declined further. The work of the miniature mass radiography service appears

to have brought forward the peaks in the annual totals which would have been expected from changes in pneumoconiosis pension schemes and levels of assessment and were in fact noted in the totals by some other industries, such as foundries and steel dressing where the sharp rise came in 1954. Thus the rise appears to have been initiated mainly by the work of the miniature mass radiography unit and temporarily maintained at a high level by the changes in schemes and assessments. The rise in the number of assessments for pneumoconiosis pensions attributable to the pottery industry was accompanied by a high average disability (appendix 3. 2a) and a slightly higher average duration of exposure (Appendix 3. 2b).

Although the diagnosed cases of category 1 simple pneumoconiosis would not normally qualify for pension, when accompanied by active tuberculosis the assessed disability would usually be reckoned as 100%, thus a reduction in the incidence of tuberculosis could also reduce the number of assessments for pneumoconiosis. In recent years only 3% of the cases were assessed as 100% as compared with 8% in 1953-54 (Appendix 3. 2a).

At one time tuberculosis was more prevalent among pottery workers (Gloyne 1951) than among the population at large and variation between the various branches of the North Staffs pottery industry was revealed by the survey in 1957 (Posner, 1957). The high incidence rate generally coincided with the high dust risk and it is particularly noteworthy that as compared with the serious mortality from silicosis and tuberculosis amongst china placers and biscuit warehouse workers who had used flint for bedding, no case of active tuberculosis was found amongst workers who had been exposed to alumina dust only. The number of annual notifications reported nationally to the Department of Health and Social Security has demonstrated a steady decline from a peak of over 40,000 cases in 1946 to less than 2,000 in 1969.

Rate of dust intake

When respirable dust[1] is inhaled a proportion of the particles penetrate into the lungs where they remain. A slight accumulation of dust in the lungs which the body cannot reject by natural processes is identifiable as dust reticulation which produces no disease or disability. The further intake of dust with pathological reaction results in impairment of the lung function and can be diagnosed as the early stages of pneumoconiosis. Additional dust intake with further bodily reaction produces further impairment giving a progression through the categories of simple pneumoconiosis to a degree of severity causing disability or even death. The categorisation from dust reticulation to the most advanced forms of pneumoconiosis is largely determined by means of X-rays now assessed in accordance with the International Labour Organisation standardisation procedure (International Labour Office, 1959).

The amount of dust required to produce silicosis in any particular individual is thought to vary on account of difference in susceptability. Attempts have been made to estimate the cumulative quantity of silica dust in the respirable size range which would be expected to cause pneumoconiosis in only a small proportion of workers exposed to the dust over their whole working life. This estimate was used by HM Factory Inspectorate to derive a suggested limit of 40 ppcc of total pottery dust which has now been replaced by the Threshold Limit Value* of 0.1 mg/m³, (Department of Employment 1970a) which is more appropriate to gravimetric determinations.[2]. The same figure of 40 ppcc was accepted by the B Ceram. RA as a practicable limit attainable with effective dust control devices and was specified in the First Report.

The cumulative intake of silica depends upon the total dust concentration, the proportion of free silica and the period of exposure. As the concentration is reduced so the period of exposure has to be extended to achieve the same total dust intake. Incomplete records of dust concentrations in the various branches of the pottery industry prevents any accurate assessment of actual improvements, but where the free silica has been eliminated or the proportion reduced the beneficial effect has been striking.

This is illustrated in the reduction in cases probably attributable to the use of siliceous material for bedding bone china (Posner and Kennedy, 1967), batwash in various branches and for polishing, from 47 in the period 1950-59 to 6 in the following decade. Changes in techniques have also contributed to reductions in total dust by elimination of particularly hazardous processes including the production and handling of dry ground flint as a raw material, in the methods of preparation and conveying dust for tile pressing, and more recently, the development of wet sponging to replace dry towing of domestic flatware. The improvement in dust control

---

* TLV refers to airborne concentrations of substances and represents conditions under which it is believed that nearly all workers may be repeatedly exposed day after day without adverse effect. Because of wide variation in individual susceptibility however, a small percentage of workers may experience discomfort from some substances at concentrations at or below the threshold. A smaller percentage may be affected more seriously by aggravation of a pre-existing condition, or by development of an occupational illness.

18

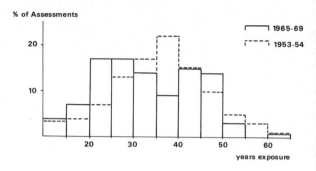

Figure 3b. Assessments for Pneumoconiosis pensions in the North Staffs pottery industry. Distribution by years of exposure 1953-54 and 1965-69

at processes where dust continues to be evolved has been particularly marked in the past ten years and should by now be influencing the annual totals.

The initial effect of any slowing down in the rate of dust inhalation should be a lengthening of the period of exposure before first assessment but this is not apparent from the comparison of the duration of exposure of cases in 1953 and 1954 with the cases from 1965-69, the most widely spaced period giving roughly the same number of cases as is illustrated in fig. 3b. Although the average duration of exposure in the ealier period was prolonged by late diagnosis, as indicated by the higher average disability (appendix 3. 2a), the high proportion of less than 30 years exposure cases for 1965-69 is disappointing as the dust exposure of those victims was almost entirely post war.

The lengthening of this 'incubation' period might also be expected from any reduction in hours worked during each year of exposure. Shorter working weeks and longer holidays would extend the period in some cases sufficiently for the worker to be removed from the hazard by retirement on resignation before the onset of pneumoconiosis. This influence would be reinforced by any breaks in employment which tend to age the working population, without a corresponding increase in exposure to dust. Such breaks could be expected to arise from the 1914-18 and 1939-45 wars, from contraction during the 1930s and to male workers from the compulsory National Service which discontinued in 1961. In the case of female workers breaks commonly occur on account of marriage and pregnancies. On the other hand, early diagnosis would tend to shorten the incubation' period. Data is not yet available to assess the relative effect of any break in employment of

Figure 3c. Assessments for Pneumoconiosis pensions in the North Staffs pottery industry. Distribution by age at assessment 1953-54 and 1965-69

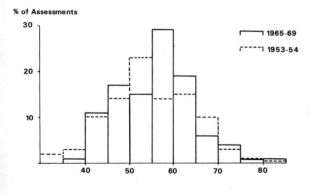

possible reduction in the rate of dust intake but their influence may be noted in the constancy of the average age on diagnosis but with a shorter average exposure while the average disability has been halved.

The effects of the changes in the schemes and levels of assessment, the miniature mass X-ray surveys and in processes and materials can be neither distinguished nor quantified, but they undoubtedly combine to make the annual totals between 1953 and 1958 artificially high, with artificially low levels during the periods immediately before and afterwards. This distortion obstructs the attempt to derive encouragement from a comparison of the total number of assessments for any one year or period with another.

However, some tentative conclusions can be drawn from the comparison of proportions of the cases attributed to the various branches of the pottery industry in two decades, 1950-59 and 1960-69. This comparison for the industrial categories previously considered in the First Report is given in table 6 and the similar comparison of proportions amongst clay shop workers shown in table 7 a, b and c.

Table 6. Assessments for pneumoconiosis pensions attributable to work in the North Staffs pottery industry 1950-1959 and 1960-1969

All workers

		1950-1959		1960-1969	
		Total	%	Total	%
1.	Milling & glaze preparation	43	2.8	14	3.7
2.	Sliphouses				
	a. Earthenware	15	1.0	5	1.3
	b. China	5	.3	3	.8
	c. Other	12	.7	2	.5
		32	2.1	10	2.6
3.	Dust Preparation	13	.8	3	.8
4.	Clay shops	910	58.2	206	54.5
5.	Biscuit placing				
	a. Earthenware	37	2.4	8	2.1
	b. China	36	2.3	4	1.1
	c. Other	33	2.1	12	3.1
		106	6.8	24	6.3
6.	Biscuit warehouse	42	3.4	13	3.4
7.	Glazing & glost placing	76	4.9	25	6.5
8.	Glost warehouse (incl. glost polishing)	35	2.3	5	1.3
9.	Decorating				
10.	Misc. occupations	51	3.9	9	2.3
11.	Mixed occupations	233	15.1	72	18.6
		1541	100	381	100
12.	Mixed industrial exposure (not included)	623		70	

Table 7. Assessments for Pneumoconiosis pensions attributable to work in the North Staffs pottery industry 1950-1959 and 1960-1969

Clay shop workers

a. ALL CLAY SHOPS

	1950-1959		1960-1969	
	Total	%	Total	%
a. Sanitary earthenware	104	11	23	11
b. Sanitary fireclay	11	1	2	1
c. Tiles (Press shops only)	117	13	10	5
d. Earthenware	546	59	134	65
e. China	79	9	16	8
f. Elec. Porcelain	20	2	10	5
g. Mixed	33	4	11	5
TOTALS	910	100	206	100

b. EARTHENWARE CLAY SHOPS

	1950-1959		1960-1969	
	Total	%	Total	%
1. Throwers & Assistants	8	1	1	1
2. Makers	220	40	47	35
3. Casters, Fettlers & spongers	101	18	26	21
4. Turners & Assistants	4	0.5	6	5
5. Other clay shop & mixed	144	26	47	35
6. Towers	69	13	7	5
TOTALS	546	100	134	100

c. CHINA CLAY SHOPS

	1950-1959		1960-1969	
	Total	%	Total	%
1. Throwers & Assistants	18	23	3	19
2. Makers	22	28	5	31
3. Casters, fettlers & spongers	4	5	2	12
4. Turners & Assistants	22	28	3	19
5. Other clay shop & mixed	13	16	3	19
TOTALS	79	100	16	100

The proportion of assessments among workers in processes up to clay shaping and in subsequent glazing and glost placing has increased, while those attributed to work in clay shops have decreased. The major reason for this variation in distribution by process is the restriction of the periodic and initial examinations to particular scheduled processes. The effect of the expansion in regular medical examination under the pneumoconiosis compensation scheme was greater in the case of clay shop workers but the distinction has now diminished as a result of the coverage by the miniature mass X-ray services. The figures for clay shop workers (table 7) reveal a reduction in the proportion of cases among towers indicating the benefits derived from improved dust control of those processes, but benefit from the use of the improved fettling hood in domestic earthenware manufacturing is not demonstrated. While there has been a reduction in the proportion of cases attributable to china turning, no doubt the result of mechanisation with improved dust control, there has been an increase in assessments amongst workers turning earthenware, normally by hand without dust control. These cases add urgency to the need for the elimination of the unsatisfactory conditions associated with hand turning. In making this comparison of the distribution of cases amongst the categories of products and occupations, the influence of changes in relative proportions of the number of workers, or more particularly in the relative number of workers who may be considered at risk on account of employment in an occupation which involves exposure to dust, must be ignored. Furthermore, the effects of variation in rates of labour turnover (Ministry of Labour and National Service 1959), which would also change the distribution of assessments, cannot be estimated at this stage. It is anticipated that at least some of these uncertainties will be resolved by the Medical Survey which has been undertaken by HM Factory Inspectorate.

This survey, which included respiratory function tests as well as full chest X-rays, covered all workers in a group of factories randomly selected from all British potteries so giving a statistically valid sample. It is anticipated that the survey will confirm the progress believed to have been made already and assist in establishing the most beneficial direction for future efforts. A firm basis for future comparison will also be provided.

Recommendations

Variables surrounding past pneumoconiosis statistics detract from their usefulness and emphasise the need for more comprehensive and systematic medical supervision. While the recent survey carried out by HM Factory Inspectorate will give statistically based guidance for future action there is still a need for the employees themselves to be considered individually. The establishment of a biological monitoring system instead of depending on voluntary mass X-rays or incomplete cover by the Pneumoconiosis Medical Panel would be welcomed.

Accidents

In 1957 The Factory Inspectorate in Stoke-on-Trent began collecting particulars of reported* accidents occurring in the pottery industry for the information of the Joint Standing Committee. Up to 1961 this information related to all British pottery manufacturers but from 1962 only the figures for the Stoke-on-Trent District of HM Factory Inspectorate were included. These figures, given in appendix 3.3, may be influenced by extraneous factors unrelated to true incidence of accidents and so must be viewed with caution. Nevertheless, the increase in reported accidents, as expressed in numbers per thousand workers, reveals a rise of 2½ times between 1957 and 1969.

The annual incidence of accidents reported by the North Staffs pottery industry compared with the corresponding figure for all British potteries is illustrated in fig. 4.

The largest single rise occurred in 1964 and coincided with a special investigation in 1964 into the non-reporting of accidents which was carried out by HM Factory Inspectorate with the result that a greater proportion of accidents may have been reported. This same influence would have been expected to contribute to the rise in reported pottery accidents. Between 1959 and 1969 the number of reported accidents in all British pottery factories increased by 66% compared with 81% for the manufacturing industry as a whole.

Of special interest is the fall in all British pottery accidents in 1962 (Appendix 3.3). The subsequent rise suggests that this temporary reduction was not achieved by any real and lasting improvement in safety standards; the main reason for the fall in 1962 might be found in the changed rates of production at that time (Machin

*Reported accidents are those resulting in disablement for more than three days and have been reported to HM Inspector of Factories in pursuance of Section 80 of the Factories Act, 1961.

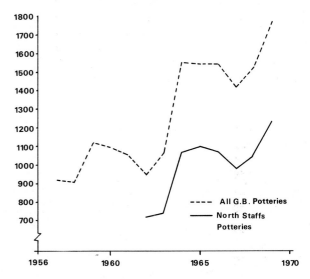

Figure 4. Annual reported accident incidence 1957-69 North Staffs and all GB Potteries

Over the same 13 year period, the total of all reported accidents in British factories rose, with fluctuations, from 150,000 to 267,000. (Department of Employment 1952-1970)

and Smyth, 1970). National manufacturing output from all industries continued to rise at a fast rate but the level of British pottery output evened out in the early 1960s and in the domestic pottery section, the principal employer, output fell fairly substantially. If the accident figures could be re-calculated to relate to the shorter hours which must have been worked during that period, some of the fluctuations in the chart (fig. 4) might well disappear.

The total of reported accidents cannot be related to the hours actually worked in order to provide a good basis for comparison between industries, but a comparison can be attempted using the incidence of reported accidents per 1,000 workers as given each year in the annual report of HM Chief Inspector of Factories. Equivalent figures for selected industries based on estimates of the numbers at risk are given in table 8. Although the figures for the North Staffordshire pottery industry are fairly low in the overall table, it is disappointing to find that they are higher than some industries such as vehicle manufacturing or engineering and electrical goods manufacturing, despite the vast difference in the degree of mechanisation and expected potential risk. It might be expected that the pottery industry accident figures would correspond more closely to other less mechanised industries, where the incidence rate is only 8 per 1,000 employees.

During the 11 year period 1959 to 1969 the notified accidents incidence rate for all British manufacturing industry rose from 19.9 to 35.3 accidents per thousand workers as compared with an increase from 17.9 to 33.8 for the British pottery industry. During the same period the number of deaths per 100,000 persons employed averaged 1.95 for the British pottery industry as compared with 4.35 for the manufacturing industry as a whole.

Table 8. Reported accidents per 1000 workers in selected industries

1965	1966	1967	1968	Industry	1969
62	61	64	68	Metal manufacture	74
60	61	66	67	Shipbuilding and marine engineering	68
47	49	52	53	Bricks, pottery, glass & cement etc.	54
39	39	40	43	Food, drink & tobacco	45
35	34	36	38	Metal goods manufacture	41
29	30	32	33	Chemical and allied industries	34
34	34	33	32	Timber, furniture etc.	33
28	29	31	32	Other manufacturing industries	33
28	26	26	27	Potteries in Stoke-on-Trent area	33
27	27	29	30	Vehicles	32
26	26	27	28	Engineering and electrical goods	29
22	23	25	26	Paper, printing & publishing	27
24	24	24	26	Textiles	26
14	15	17	18	Laundries and repair services, garages	19
18	19	17	18	Leather and fur	18
7	7	7	8	Clothing and footwear	8

Source: 1965-69 HM Chief Inspector of Factories annual reports.

Distribution of pottery accidents by cause and nature and site of injury

The distribution of the North Staffs pottery accidents by cause category is shown in fig. 5 which also gives the comparable distribution for all British accidents in factory processes. The distribution pattern with a high proportion of handling accidents and relatively few from machinery would be expected where there is a high frequency rate coupled with rather less severity than in more mechanised industries. When classified by nature of injury (fig. 6) a high proportion of strains and sprains is revealed. While nationally one quarter of all injuries

are so classified, in the North Staffs pottery industry the proportion rises to over one third.

An analysis of accident by site of injury (fig. 7) also points to the disturbingly high rate of handling accidents. Trunk injuries in Stoke-on-Trent account for 31% of the pottery accidents as compared with the national all-industry rate of only 24% (in 1968). The excess appears to be due to the increased prevalence of strains and sprains. Seventeen (in 1968) per cent of trunk injuries resulting from accidents in all British factories are attributed to sprains and strains while a corresponding figure for the Stoke-on-Trent pottery industry is substantially higher at 23%.

Machinery Accidents

The proportion of machinery accidents among those reported (7%) is small when compared with the national figure for all factory processes (fig. 5) (average 1969, 18%) but this would be expected in an industry using largely hand work. As new or different machinery is introduced whether for production or transport, the distribution of the accidents amongst the categories of machines could change.

A changing pattern is in fact revealed by an examination of the accidents occurring at various machines as indicated in appendix 3.8. The actual number of accidents at a particular machine has little significance as it cannot be related to the machine population, but a guide as to the changes in incidence is given by comparing the number of accidents for the five year periods 1957-61 and 1965 to 1969. Whereas a reduction in the later periods could have resulted from the exclusion of the 'out-pottery' accidents any apparent increase would be specially interesting. This comparison (table 9) reveals that the machines showing an increased number of accidents are all characteristic of increasing mechanisation and include some machines of recent introduction to the industry.

The statutory responsibility for providing protection at most dangerous parts of machinery is placed upon the user of the machine even though the machine may be newly manufactured. Efforts have been made to assist machine manufacturers in satisfactorily guarding all dangerous parts of new machines before offering them for use in the pottery industry and progress is now becoming apparent. An example of design safety is given by the modifications made by one manufacturer to a machine having one of the most common mechanical motions in domestic pottery ware manufacturing — the 'nodding' making head as illustrated in fig. 8.

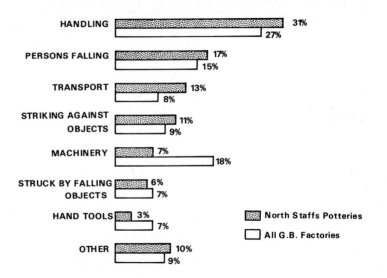

Figure 5. Reported factory accidents. North Staffs potteries 1967-69 and all GB factory processes 1969.

Distribution by cause

	North Staffs Potteries	All G.B. Factories
HANDLING	31%	27%
PERSONS FALLING	17%	15%
TRANSPORT	13%	8%
STRIKING AGAINST OBJECTS	11%	9%
MACHINERY	7%	18%
STRUCK BY FALLING OBJECTS	6%	7%
HAND TOOLS	3%	7%
OTHER	10%	9%

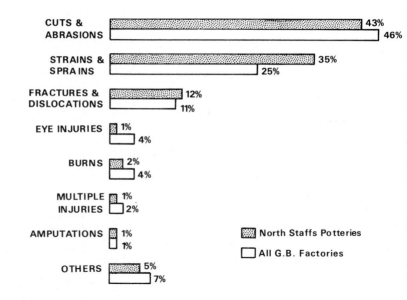

Figure 6. Reported factory accidents North Staffs potteries 1967-69 and all GB factory processes.

Distribution by nature of inquiry

	North Staffs Potteries	All G.B. Factories
CUTS & ABRASIONS	43%	46%
STRAINS & SPRAINS	35%	25%
FRACTURES & DISLOCATIONS	12%	11%
EYE INJURIES	1%	4%
BURNS	2%	4%
MULTIPLE INJURIES	1%	2%
AMPUTATIONS	1%	1%
OTHERS	5%	7%

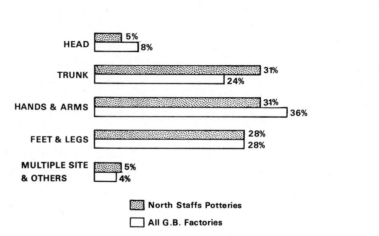

Figure 7. Reported factory accidents North Staffs potteries 1967-69 and all GB factory processes.

Distribution by site of injury

	North Staffs Potteries	All G.B. Factories
HEAD	5%	8%
TRUNK	31%	24%
HANDS & ARMS	31%	36%
FEET & LEGS	28%	28%
MULTIPLE SITE & OTHERS	5%	4%

The usual means of restricting the motion of the making head is by means of adjustment of the set screw 'A'. With the stop in this position there is clearly a possibility of trapping and accidents have in fact occurred at these parts. As a result of HM Factory Inspector's discussions with the manufacturers the machine was modified by removing the stop to position 'B' in which position the trap between the fixed and moving parts is inaccessible and the danger has been eliminated.

Machines shown in table 9 as causing an apparently decreased number of accidents include some which are being taken out of use. For example, hand or semi-automatic tile presses have now been partially replaced by fully automatic machines and at some other machines improved safeguards are now available.

The pug mill as used in nearly every pottery for converting filter press cake to homogenous plastic clay for shaping, presents danger of trapping by the rotating

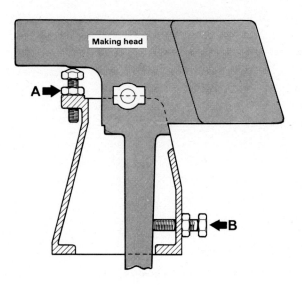

Figure 8. Sectional diagram of a Service roller making machine with the 'nodding head' at the lower limit of its travel

Table 9. Reported machinery accidents — North Staffs potteries

Totals for 1957-61 and 1965-69 by machine

Machine	1957-61	1965-69	Ratio 1965-69 / 1957-61
	a	b	c
Conveyors	14	46	3.3
Lifting	10	20	2.0
Presses — other*	17	31	1.8
— automatic	12	17	1.4
Turning	10	12	1.2
Roller making	—	7	—
Towing	—	7	—
Pan mills	14	12	.9
Semi-automatic flat	40	33	.8
cup	53	44	.8
Grinding	20	15	.8
Other	166	127	.8
Presses — semi-automatic	16	11	.7
Tile dipping	10	6	.6
Murray Curvex	12	7	.6
Sorting	10	6	.6
Pug mills	13	7	.5
Presses — hand	28	9	.4

*Mainly hydraulic presses

Compiled from appendix 3.8

Note: The figures given in col. a include all British pottery reported accidents but col. b relate only to those in the North Staffordshire area.

worm against the inside of the machine casing. This dangerous trap situated at the base of the feed hopper is necessarily approached when feeding, especially when pushing the clay down to the worm or during cleaning. Accidents at these parts can result in serious injury.

Improved standards of safeguarding may have contributed to the apparent reduction in pug mill accidents but these machines are still sometimes found in use with inadequate safety precautions.

The safeguard provided should enable the clay to be fed into the feed hopper but must prevent a worker from reaching the dangerous trap. At horizontal pugs this is most commonly achieved by an extension to the feed hopper of the type illustrated in fig. 9. A B C & D. The hopper extension may be designed to prevent access by eliminating all possibility of direct approach or by ensuring that all points of access around the extended feed hopper are so far removed as to eliminate the possibility of reaching the trapping point. In the former case the hopper extension incorporates a fixed top, while in the latter case, care must be exercised to ensure that the safeguard is not defeated by a worker standing on a raised platform or part of the machine casing. The hopper extension shown in fig. 9B has a trip bar fitted to its front edge for emergency stopping of the machine.

In a few instances, e.g., at small extrusion pugs where narrow strips of clay cut from the pressed cake are fed into the machine, a series of fixed bars at the top of the existing hopper will suffice if so spaced as to prevent access of the fingers to the dangerous part, but still permit the passage of clay. This type of guard is illustrated in fig. 9E & G. If the bars cannot be spaced to prevent access, it may be possible to provide a narrow feed opening at a greater distance above the dangerous part by the method illustrated in fig. 9F.

Where guards have to be removed for cleaning and so cannot be permanently attached to the machine, interlocking arrangements are necessary to prevent the machine from being set in motion before the guard is replaced. The most common interlocking arrangement is the provision of a magnetically operated switch attached to the machine case with the operating magnet fixed to the guard so that the electrical supply is interrupted when the guard is removed. A suitable arrangement is illustrated in fig. 9G.

Figure 9. Methods of preventing access to the worm of pug mills

In one factory difficulties in cleaning were encountered when the guards were interlocked as the machine could not be turned manually. In that case it was found possible to fit a turning handle as illustrated in fig. 10.

Vertical pugs are now relatively rare and normally found only in small potteries. As yet no satisfactory method of guarding these machines has been devised and consequently previous users have tended to purchase ready pugged clay or to instal a small horizontal pug for which standard guards are available.

Transport and kiln accidents

During the period 1957-1969 there has been a very marked rise in transport accidents: this is illustrated in fig. 11. The total number of transport accidents in the North Staffs potteries from 1965-1969 was more than double the number for all British potteries in a similar period from 1957-1961. This increase reflects the extending use of mechanical transport in an industry which hitherto has depended very largely on hand carrying of ware during the various stages of manufacture. If the upward trend in transport accidents is to be halted, greater care will be required in the design and introduction of mechanical transportation systems.

One of the reasons for the high proportion of transport accidents in the North Staffs potteries (13%) as compared with all British industry (8%) as indicated in fig. 5, is the unusually high proportion involving rail transport, 30% of all transport accidents as compared with an all British industry figure of about 10%. Rail transport in potteries is principally concerned with

Figure 10. Hand turning a pug for cleaning

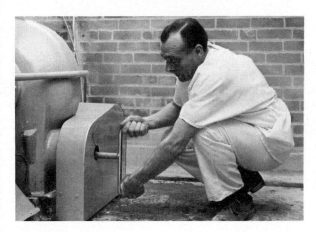

Figure 12a. Lowering a kiln car for ease of unloading

Figure 11. Reported Transport Accidents 1957-1969

North Staffs potteries

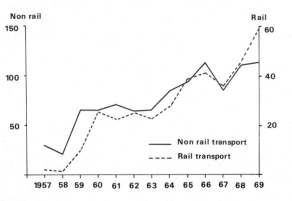

tunnel kiln operations and the number of these accidents have risen with the growing use of such kilns.

An analysis of a group of accidents associated with the use of kiln trucks revealed four main hazards (Wainwright and Evans, 1969) for each of which a remedy was available even if not frequently applied. These are tabulated in table 10.

Although new kiln installations normally provide for low slung trucks, so avoiding the step of up to 0.5 m between the level of the kiln and the transfer rails, the other precautions are relatively rare. Where remedies have been applied the motive has not only been the elimination of danger but also the desire for more efficient production and it is hoped that closer examination of kiln operations will induce more potteries to adopt the same modifications in the joint interests of safety and production.

Explosions and other accidents arising from the use of gas at kilns and other gas fired plant were relatively rare and those incidents which did occur would normally have been averted by the scrupulous observance of the earlier JSC Recommendations (Joint Standing Committee for the Pottery Industry, 1960). Consideration is being given to the need for revision of that advice to take account of the change to natural or liquified petroleum gas. It would be desirable to standardise safeguards at gas fired plant and to establish a system of regular inspection by a competent person to ensure that the appropriate safeguards are not only provided but also satisfactorily maintained. Such an inspection service could be on the lines of that already applied statutorily in the case of pressure vessels and lifting equipment, and adopted voluntarily by many firms in respect of their electrical equipment and other plant.

Figure 12b. Kiln car lowered for ease of unloading

Table 10. Accidents associated with kiln transport

Operation	Hazard	Remedy
Kiln car loading	Strains due to lifting and reaching	Lower car into truck for loading at constant level (fig. 12)
Car and transfer truck moving	Strains due to pushing heavy trucks	Mechanical assistance
Pulling transfer trucks	Wheels over toes	Wheel guards (fig. 13)
Personnel access	Falling from one level to another	Low slung trucks

Figure 13. Wheel protector at a kiln transfer truck

Handling accidents

The causation and injury distribution of North Staffs pottery accidents suggested that a significant reduction in total accidents could readily be achieved by an examination of all the lifting and handling operations in the industry with a view to determining which of them could more safely be accomplished by mechanical means and which loads could be broken down into smaller units less likely to cause injury.

Recent installations of overhead and roller conveyors, load levelling devices, the introduction of fork lift trucks and partial mechanisation of scrap return are potential means of reducing handling accidents and at the same time bringing improvements in productivity.

In addition to the rise in transport accidents, conveyors and lifting machines have also caused an increasing number of accidents in potteries (appendix 3.8). Accidents at conveyors in North Staffs potteries during the five year period from 1956 to 1969 totalled 46 as compared with 14 in all British potteries during a similar period from 1957 to 1961; lifting machine accidents rose from 10 to 20 during the same period.

An indication of the expected effect of mechanisation of handling is suggested by the study of handling accidents in all British factories during an eight year period from 1950 (Department of Employment, 1957-1970). This study reported by HM Chief Inspector of Factories revealed a steady reduction amounting to about 25% in the incidence of handling accidents at a time when mechanisation increased as indicated by a slight rise in transport accidents. This trend has not been observed in the North Staffs pottery industry where although mechanisation is increasing with a corresponding rise in transport accidents there is no compensating reduction in other categories of accidents.

In an effort to identify some of the characteristics of handling accidents in potteries a half of all accidents of this category reported to HM Factory Inspectorate by North Staffs potteries during the last quarter of 1969 were investigated and the findings and recommendations are noted below.

This enquiry related only to 'reportable' accidents so excluding all minor cuts and abrasions which could result from the handling of biscuit or other abrasive materials. Believing that many minor, and hence unreportable, accidents result from the handling of abrasive ware, a recommendation was sent to all manufacturers in August 1970 (Joint Standing Committee for the Pottery Industry, 1970a) that they make protective finger stalls or gloves available on request to operatives engaged in work which could cause soreness or injury.

Table 11. Reported accidents in the Stoke-on-Trent district (figures in brackets give percentage of total)

	Pottery			Other Industries		
	Handling	Non Handling	Total	Handling	Non Handling	Total
Last quarter 1969	113 (28)	199 (72)	312	193 (32)	419 (68)	612
All 1969	420 (30)	832 (70)	1,252	695 (35)	1,754 (65)	2,449

Table 12. Distribution of handling accidents among factories by size

Factory size	No of Factories	Accidents		Workers	
		No	%	No	%
1-50	87	1	2	1,093	3
51-200	65	9	18	7,988	21
201-500	47	19	37	14,315	36
over 500	19	22	43	14,943	39
Total	218	51	100	38,339	100

Table 13. Distribution of accidents in product groups

Product Group	Accidents		Workers	
	No	%	No (thousands)	%
Sanitary fireclay	2	4	.5	1
Vit. china	4	8	1.3	3
	6	12	1.8	4
Domestic E'Ware	22	44	17.7	46
Bone China	3	6	5.7	15
Mixed	4	8	4.6	11
	29	58	28.0	72
Tiles Fireclay	—	—	.6	2
E'ware	7	14	3.7	10
	7	14	4.3	12
Industrial Fireclay	1	2	.7	2
E'Ware	6	12	2.2	6
	7	14	2.9	8
Materials — Mills	1	2	.6	2
Glazes	1	2	.6	2
	2	4	1.2	4
Totals	51	100	38.3	100

28

Survey of handling accidents

During the last quarter of 1969, 113 handling accidents were reported to HM District Inspector of Factories by the pottery industry in North Staffs. Of these, alternate reports were taken on order of receipt for investigation giving a sample of 56. Of these, two were found not to be reportable and three others excluded because they did not arise from pottery processes but from construction work or employment away from the premises. Although the proportion of handling accidents in North Staffs potteries is higher than for all British factory processes, it is lower than for the other industries in the Stoke-on-Trent district. In the last quarter of 1969 the handling accidents represented 28% of the total reportable pottery accidents and 32% for other industries in the Stoke-on-Trent district during the same period. The equivalent annual percentages were 30% and 35% respectively (table 11).

This proportion of handling accidents amongst all accidents reported by Stoke-on-Trent potteries was not significantly different from the average for the last eight years.

The expectation that handling accidents would be more prevalent in the smaller factories where mechanical aids might be less available, is not supported by the relatively constant distribution of the accidents among the size range of factories, table 12.

The apparent excess of accidents in the larger size ranges over the number expected from the proportion of workers is not statistically significant. (See also table 17).

The distribution of the accidents among the different product and occupation groups show small but significant variations from the distribution of workers. (table 13 and 14). The domestic ware section of the industry produce fewer accidents than expected, especially in bone china and mixed production but there is a disproportionate number of accidents among those producing the heavier and more difficult to handle sanitary ware. The number of accidents per 1,000 workers was also above average in the industrial earthenware (mainly electro ceramics) and the wall tile sections of the industry.

The difference between distribution of accidents and workers among the process department of potteries is also statistically significant. As would be expected from the nature of the work, glazing and decorating account for relatively few accidents but the 17% of the workers in the warehouse and packing department where there is much handling of heavy containers share 38% of the accidents.

The sections and process departments of the industry showing higher than expected incidence of handling accidents appear to be those in which heavy or awkward loads have to be moved, although the provision of handling aids such as conveyors, fork lift or tug lift trucks and other mechanisation should tend to make handling accidents more uniform across the industry. The difference revealed indicates where effort to reduce the number of accidents might be most fruitful.

No enquiries were made into the loss to production resulting from these accidents, but it would not be unreasonable to suppose that the losses caused by all accidents regardless of any incidence of injury could be

Table 14. Distribution by department

Department	Accidents No	%	Workers No (thousands)	%
Preparation	3	6	.6	2
Sliphouse	2	4	.9	3
Making	15	30	10.3	27
Firing	3	6	.7	2
Glazing & decorating	4	8	10.9	28
Warehouse & packing	19	38	6.7	17
Other	5	10	8.2	21
Totals	51	100	38.3	100

Table 15. Distribution of accident by site and nature of injury

Nature of Injury	Head	Site of Injury Trunk	Arm/ hand	Foot/ leg	Total	%
Fractures and dislocations		1	2	4	7	14
Sprains & strains		30		3	33	66
Open wounds			3		3	6
Bruising & crushing			2	1	3	6
Foreign body			1		1	2
Burns						
Other injury	1		3		4	8
Total	1	31	11	8	51	100
%	2	62	22	16		

reduced and productivity improved by a review of handling methods.

The need for such review may also be indicated by the distribution of the 'nature of injury' classification. The vast majority, 62%, of handling accidents caused injury to the trunk with a further 22% of hand and arm injuries (table 15) while the division by nature of the injury revealed sprains and strains as the major single type (table 15). Only one of the trunk injuries (dislocated shoulder) was not attributed to a sprain or strain.

Handling accidents do not arise from the occasional and abnormal work which might attract special risk. Only one of the 51 accidents occurred when performing an operation not constituting a routine part of the normal production work and in 44 instances the weight of the object being handled was estimated to have been within the normal capacity of the worker. Two accidents occurred while dragging loads which were clearly beyond the capacity of the worker while five were apparently attributable to attempting to move objects which may have been within the capacity of two men. Thus there is seen to be a need to simplify and ease the normal day to day as well as the exceptional handling of work. In only one instance was any suitable mechanical assistance available at the time of the accident.

Although the number of workers engaged in the handling of finished ware is small, the reported handling accidents attributed to this work amounted to 30%. It is possible that part of the explanation lies in the increasing popularity of container packing which leads to more handling operations of bulky and sometimes heavy loads. Handling accidents tended to be regarded as trivial with the result that management often failed to make any investigation to establish the cause and so consider appropriate remedies. Although 17 of the 51 accidents were investigated to some extent, there were marked variations in the proportion of accidents investigated by management in the different sections of the industry. In domestic ware manufacturing as a whole 10 of the 29 accidents were investigated, giving the same proportion as the overall average, but six of the seven accidents in bone china and mixed manufacturing categories, where the incidence rate also compared favourably, were investigated. Similarly there was a low proportion of investigations in the wall tile and industrial earthenware manufacturing where the incidence rates were above average. Factory size appears to have some influence on the frequency of investigation (table 16). The percentage investigated in the over 500 employed size range is depressed by the fact that 15 of the 22, or 30% of the total, occurred in only four of the

Table 16. Investigated handling accidents by factory size

Factory Size	No of Accidents	No Investigated	% Investigated
1-200	10	1	10
201-500	19	8	42
over 500	22	8	36
Total	51	17	34

Table 17. Incidence of all accidents per 100 workers (in 36 factories)

	Range of incidence rates 100 workers	Average number of workers
1st quartile	5-14	774
2nd quartile	15-25	562
3rd quartile	26-40	367
4th quartile	45-83	247

factories in this size group, i.e. about 25% of the size range or 2.5 of all North Staffs potteries.

Although 66% of the accidents were not investigated, 74% occurred in factories where there was a safety committee and 76% where there was a safety officer. Twenty six per cent occurred in potteries where there was no safety promotion scheme other than the occasional use of posters.

It appears that accidents may be concentrated not only in some particular sections and departments, but also in particular factories and that effective safety organisation, coupled with accident investigation, could make a significant contribution to safer working conditions. On the other hand there are no indications that the designation of an employee as safety officer will in itself bring any benefit, although such an appointment is clearly regarded as a useful extension of the safety committee activities.

The rate of incidence of all accidents, including those which were not reportable, was determined in 36 of the 41 factories in which records were kept. Incidence rates per 100 workers varies from 5 to 83 with a median of 25. It is interesting to note the lower incidence figures in the larger factories, (table 17).

The reason for this great variation in incidence rate and apparent relationship to factory size would seem to be worthy of further study.

Accident Prevention

In the past, considerations of worker safety have tended to be over-shadowed by problems of health. Works Inspectors appointed under the Regulations and trained at the North Staffs Polytechnic* have been given some instruction on general safety but very few of them will have been given any opportunity for further training in general safety or acquiring experience.

When a national survey was carried out in February 1967 it was found that 18% of the factories in which more than 50 persons were employed had Joint Safety Committees. In addition there were factories with joint committees of management and workers which dealt with safety as well as other matters and this brought up to 37% the proportion of factories in which there was some joint consultation on safety. There was considerable variation from industry to industry; vehicle manufacturers having an accident incidence rate only just above that for the pottery industry had joint consultation on safety in more than half of the factories employing over 50 workers. Engineering and electrical goods manufacturers had nearly the same proportion of factory joint consultation and achieved an accident incidence rate as low as that in the relatively low risk pottery industry.

In contrast to this in Stoke-on-Trent there was joint consultation on safety matters in no more than 5% of the 140 potteries in which more than 50 were then employed. (Wainwright and Evans, 1969). At that time among the North Staffs pottery manufacturers there was no known safety officer as such although in some factories the responsibility for safety was shared with other duties. There is now a welcome recognition of the importance of safety and some of the bigger manufacturers have extended the duties of the Works Inspector to cover general safety.

Recommendations

No new machine should be brought into use until all appropriate safeguards are provided. To this end users are recommended to order machines complete with adequate protection and machine manufacturers should ensure that safety is integrated into the basic design. The assistance of HM Factory Inspectorate in establishing a satisfactory standard of protection, together with means of indicating when it has been reached, would encourage this progress and assist in ensuring that new mechanical hazards are not introduced. Before a new machine is brought into use, checks should be made to ensure that all necessary safeguards are properly fitted.

Where improved standards of safety are devised for new machines, modifications should be made available, wherever possible, to existing machine users. Means of propagating information about new or improved safety techniques to machine makers and users should be sought, possibly to cover dust protection and other related matters as well as mechanical safety.

Handling of finished ware, as well as material, in the course of production should be examined to establish where mechanical assistance could reduce the likelihood of accidents. Where such mechanisation is introduced special care is required to ensure that no additional hazards are created. When appropriate, gloves or other hand protection should be made available.

Where mechanical assistance is neither practicable nor justified, the work should be so arranged and conducted by employees that the hazard of sprains and strains is minimised. Training in lifting, together with appropriate posters would assist.

In each factory a person of sufficient seniority should be specifically charged with the duty of promoting safety. In practice the extension of the works inspector's duties and training to include general safety would normally be possible. The function of such a person should include the investigation of accidents with a view to eliminating their cause and other similar hazards. Employees should co-operate fully in the efforts to promote safe working conditions and bring to the notice of management without delay any defects in safeguards or suggested means of improving standards.

*Previously the North Staffordshire College of Technology.   1, 2   Part 4 Dust Measuring

Problems
Identified

Significant changes in the various branches of the industry have taken place during the past few decades, many of them affecting the potential risk of pneumoconiosis. The divisions of the industry are considered separately in an effort to identify those changes which have been specially beneficial and to consider how they might be more widely applied.

Flint Milling

Within a few years of its first use in pottery manufacture, flint was recognised as a hazard on account of the dust which was produced and breathed into the lungs. This recognition quickly led to substitution of wet for dry grinding in order that all the "said Hazards and Inconveniences attending the same will effectually be prevented." (Meiklejohn, 1969). These hazards and inconveniences had been described in the 18th century as proving "very destructive to mankind, inasmuch as any person ever so healthful and strong working in that business cannot probably survive for 2 years."

Although increasingly effective improvements made over many years have dramatically reduced the hazard, new assessments for pneumoconiosis have continued to arise amongst mill workers[1]. The average disability in the new cases assessed among mill workers during the past decade was not significantly different from that for all pottery cases, but the average period of exposure before first diagnosis was 24 years as compared with an all cases average of 35 years. The incidence rate amongst mill workers as compared with other parts of the industry cannot be reliably estimated until relative rates of labour turnover are determined.

The enhanced risk as indicated by the shorter period of exposure might be expected in that part of the industry dealing with the hazardous ingredient of pottery body in its separate state. For many years this fact has been recognised and considerable improvements in dust levels have been achieved, but recent investigations, including examination of plant under Tyndall beam lighting, have revealed that dust control was frequently ineffective and attempts at wetting reduced, but did not eliminate, the evolution of dust.

While such materials as flint or sand continue to be used in pottery manufacture, and thus have to be processed, a very high standard of operational safety is imperative. Ideally the whole of the preparatory processes from receipt of the raw material to preparation of slop ground silica should be carried on entirely within a closed system.

While the labour force in the milling industry, and the number of factories engaged in milling operations have declined[2], the throughput of flint has risen with the increasing output of pottery, although in recent years there has developed a trend for partial substitution of sand for flint. This marked increase in throughput per worker and more specially per plant, has been achieved by increasing mechanisation which has made possible the partial realisation of the concept of closed circuit production. The number of workers actually at risk and the time of their potential exposure to atmospheric dust have both been reduced.

In the case of sand this standard of operational safety can be more readily achieved through pneumatic handling techniques than is possible with flint, which has to be subjected to many more processes including calcining, crushing and screening, each stage in turn being linked by elevators, chutes or conveyors. Considerable progress has been made in modifying production methods so as to facilitate enclosure and dust control, but regular transportation of calcined crushed flint to separate milling plant gives rise to

Figure 14. Typical flint processing plant

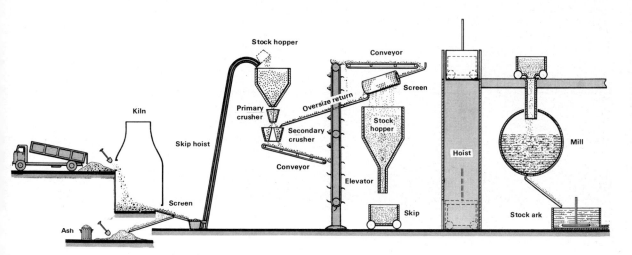

difficulties in providing efficient dust control. Closed circuit production can in effect continue from the mill to the pottery by containing the material within water, but any drying of the slop to enable the material to be handled as filter press cake or semi-dry lumps as loose bulk material should be avoided unless equivalent containment can be achieved.

It has been reported (Department of Employment, 1970a) that cristobalite should be reckoned as more harmful than quartz and a weighting factor of 2 is applied in arriving at the Threshold Limit Value[3]. Flint is normally calcined to give a cristobalite content of up to about 10% making a quartz equivalent* of about 110%. Where raw sand is substituted there is a slight reduction in the intrinsic hazard but this is not the case if calcined sand with a cristobalite content of more than 10% is used. Some of the calcined sand now being introduced has a cristobalite content substantially in excess of this figure.

A traditional flint process is illustrated in fig. 14 but considerable simplification is found in new or reconstructed plant. Although variations in layout are possible, the essential stages in production include calcining, crushing and grinding with means of separating and returning for additional crushing those flints which

*Quartz equivalent is determined by the summation of the percentage free silica as quartz and twice the percentage present as cristobalite or tridymite.

Figure 15. Picking out uncalcined flints ordinary lighting

Figure 16. Picking out uncalcined flints Tyndall beam lighting

are oversize. In the absence of efficient dust control these major items of plant involved in the tranformation of calcined flints into ground slop would constitute serious sources of airborne dust, as also would the means of linking them together — conveyors, chutes and elevators.

Flints are calcined by loading alternate layers of flint and coal into a vertical bottle kiln where they are fired to 950°C. for a minimum of six hours. This calcining process incinerates the organic content leaving the flints white and friable. Although this form of kiln is still used sometimes with a continuous feed of flints and fuel, new continuous oil and gas fired kilns with mechanised loading are being introduced. Unlike the handling of calcined flints at the kiln discharge point or any subsequent dry operation, manipulation of raw flints presents no risk to health.

Discharge of coal fired kilns whether continuous or discontinuous in operation requires means of separating the fuel ash from the flints which have to be fed to a skip hoist for conveyance to a calcined flint stock hopper. Kiln emptying and ash separation at older plant has been done by hand with ineffective attempts at dust suppression by wetting. More recently efforts have been made to mechanise this operation and so facilitate the provision of enclosure with exhaust draught, but so far the problem has not been completely solved. However the new type of continuous kiln using ashless fuel has been designed to discharge into a water trough from which the cooled and soaked flints are drawn by conveyor. This discharge system eliminates any emptying and skip transfer so enabling complete enclosure to be provided from the kiln discharge up to the calcined flint hopper. Maintenance of this enclosure under negative pressure would prevent any escape of airborne dust.

Transfer of the flint from the stock hopper to the first stage crusher, usually jaw crusher, is normally by means of totally enclosed chutes or conveyors, but the continuity of the closed circuit is sometimes broken at the feed point to the mill to provide facility for picking out inadequately fired flints. (figs. 15 & 16). Although not completely fired, the flints are still friable and disintegrate to give rise to dust when handled. As this practice is not universal there is some doubt as to its real necessity. Primary and secondary crushing are the principal sources of dust and these can be adequately controlled only by enclosure to contain the flint and extraction to prevent any upward flow of dusty air.

A similar standard of enclosure and dust control can be achieved at the screen and associated plant up to the filling of the crushed flint hopper. The necessity for air extraction in addition to total enclosure of all such plant has been established by Tyndall beam investigations (fig. 17) (Department of Employment and Productivity, 1969).

Figure 17. Dust escaping from an enclosed conveyor without air extraction — Tyndall beam lighting

Batch grinding in ball mills requires batch feeding of flints and this is invariably achieved by means of mobile skips running on floor or overhead rails. Novel arrangements have been devised to overcome the difficulties in controlling the dust when filling or emptying these skips. Whenever calcined crushed flints are filled into a container, dust laden air is displaced from the interior as it is filled and this must be aspirated. This applies both to the filling of the mobile skip and the charging of the cylinder mill.

The first essential is that the skip be enclosed and provision made for connection to an exhaust system whenever flint is being manipulated. Fig. 18 shows a skip at a filling point where a good attempt has been made to achieve complete dust control. The exhaust connection is completed by means of an expandable duct so designed that air is drawn into the skip with the draught induced by the inflowing material and is conducted away. A separate system to control dust evolved when filling the cylindrical mill was designed to draw air from the interior of the mill and so reinforce the air flow naturally induced by the flow of material. These two design criteria were met by the use of a concentric tundish with air extracted through the annular space (fig. 19).

Although a great improvement over former methods at the point of discharge from the mobile skip the continuity of the closed circuit was broken.

A new installation has sought to overcome this weakness by continuing an unbroken closed circuit and incorporating a single dust control system for filling and emptying the mobile skip. The same degree of enclosure of the skip is achieved, but the connection to the fixed duct for air extraction is made by a pneumatically operated telescopic duct section such that the connection is only completed if the skip rests at, and is not simply drawn past, the filling point (fig. 20). This pneumatic movement also opens a butterfly valve in the duct, thus ensuring optimum efficiency and economy in extraction. A duct integrated with the skip allows about 10% of the extracted air to be drawn from the enclosure at the emptying point where dust could otherwise leak during filling.

When emptying the skip, a similar connection is made but the ratio of extracted air from the top and bottom is reversed so as to give 90% of the extraction at the discharge enclosure, which maintains the closed circuit principle by feeding the materials via a suitably designed tundish directly into the mills below.

Similar ingenuity has been displayed in overcoming a problem of batch transfer of loose material into hoppers in the associated pottery supply industry engaged in

Figure 18. Dust control apparatus for skip filling

Figure 19. Tundish for ball mill filling with concentric air extraction

Figure 20. *Pneumatically connected air extraction duct at a skip being filled with crushed calcined flints*

glaze preparation. This dust control device depends upon a method of variable connections into a fixed extraction duct (fig. 21).

The skip is mounted on rails running across the tops of a series of in-line hoppers. The skip enclosure was fitted with a horizontal duct connection designed to fit into a slot along the fixed exhaust duct at the back of the rails. This duct was of rectangular section with the slot along the front closed by means of two overlapping rubber flaps. The terminal for the skip duct only separated the flaps at the point of entry to make connection to the exhaust system.

A similar arrangement (fig. 22) was attempted with an overhead duct above rails on which moved a mobile weigh-hopper. The canopy provided over the scale hopper is to be fitted with an enclosure to form a hood and so afford more efficient control of the dust rising from the manipulation of powders.

Figure 22. *Vertical connection from a movable hood into an air extraction duct*

Figure 21. *Horizontal connection from a movable hood into an air extraction duct*

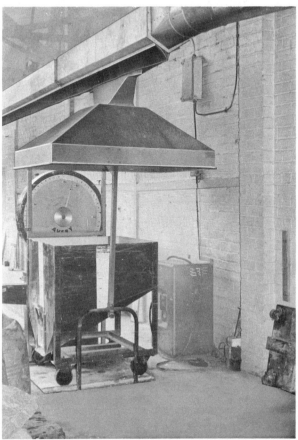

Recommendations

The aim should be to carry on all grinding and disintegration processes and conveying of material from one stage to the next entirely within a closed circuit, with adequate air extraction to prevent any possible escape of dust from the plant. Where this ideal cannot at the present be achieved, particularly on existing plant, high standards of dust control should be provided at all points where dust might otherwise be evolved.

Some of the difficulties in individual factories, of devising means of solving those problems which are common to the industry, may have been more readily overcome if a co-operative effort could have been made. It is desirable that the industry should establish machinery for the sharing of ideas at practical level and possibly the undertaking of joint development in appropriate projects.

Effective monitoring should be undertaken to ensure that the standards are properly maintained.

Tile Manufacturing

Glazed wall tiles

The wall tile* manufacturing industry uses a body with a higher free silica content than other parts of the pottery industry, usually 40 to 45% but occasionally higher. Furthermore, unlike other pottery shaping processes, dust tile pressing uses partly dried and ground body as a powder. Although developments in body composition have not led to any significant reduction in the free silica content, changes in methods of producing and using the body powder could increase operational safety in the manufacture of dust pressed wall tiles. The slip casting process using a lower free silica content body for the manufacture of once fired tiles which is used in one factory only does not present the same difficulties.

The suspected higher risk in wall tile manufacturing (Ministry of Labour and National Service, 1943) as compared with other branches of the industry as suggested in table IV of the First Report has attracted much attention in the past including the setting up of an Advisory Committee in 1938 by the Chief Inspector of Factories and the incorporation of some of its recommendations in the present Pottery Regulations

* Unless otherwise stated, wall tiles refer to glazed wall tiles shaped by dust pressing and twice fired.

Table 18. Assessments for pneumoconiosis pensions among wall tile workers by the pneumoconiosis medical panel, Stoke-on-Trent 1950-54 and 1964-68

	1950-54			1964-68		
	Average years Exposure	Average Dis- ability	No. of cases	Average years Exposure	Average Dis- ability	No. of cases
Dust Prepara- tion	28	29	8	12	10	2
Pressing and Fettling	24	17	39	20	35	5
Other	37	24	10	35	20	4

Source: Private communications from the Pneumoconiosis Medical Panel

(SI 65, 1950) and more recently, the development work of the B Ceram. RA with the subsequent recommendations contained in the First Report.

Labour turnover (Ministry of Labour and National Service, 1959) and other variable[4] prevents the absolute number of assessments for pneumoconiosis pensions among workers in the wall tile manufacturing industry from providing a reliable guide as to relative dangers. Although pneumoconiosis incidence figures for 1950 to 1954 and 1964 to 1968 are not entirely equivalent, they provide a basis for broad comparisons of exposure before first diagnosis (table 18).

The shorter period of exposure before first assessment among dust preparation workers in the later period may be partly due to earlier diagnosis as indicated by the lower average disability. On the other hand, the eight cases in 1950-54 includes one 100% assessment on account of tuberculosis and this tends to raise the average disability. Assessments of pressing and fettling workers, though fewer in number, show a slightly shorter period of exposure with twice the average disability although again this average is elevated by a 100% assessment and counting all 'less than 10%' assessments as 10%. It is of interest to note that in the early period tile manufacturing contributed 13% of the newly assessed cases but only 5% in the second decade. During this period the total output and output per worker were both substantially increased.

Dust Preparation

Although some manufacturers continue to prepare dust by grinding dried filter press cake, the majority of tile body powder is produced by drying on the surface of a heated drum rotating in a bath of prepared body; the adhering dried clay is scraped from the drum and, like the broken filter press cake, is afterwards ground and sieved. Spray dryers recently introduced and already operating in some factories convert body slip directly into dried material. The prepared dust is normally stored in hoppers before feeding to presses by belt conveyors and bucket elevators, or sometimes by means of portable containers.

The relatively few primary dust sources restricted to conveyors, elevators, tipping points and clay breaking units can be enclosed to contain the material and provided with exhaust ventilation to prevent the escape of dusty air. A far greater problem is the prevention of secondary dust such as that which arises from the material spilled on the floor, ground and disturbed by traffic to give rise to atmospheric dust. The problem of uncontrolled secondary dust sources leading to general atmospheric contamination has long been recognised. (Ministry of Labour and National Service, 1959). While some progress towards its elimination has been made

Figure 23. Spillage container formed from a conveyor enclosure being emptied by vacuum

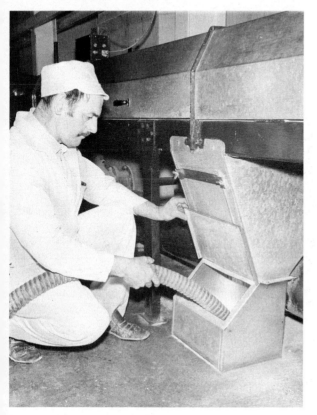

further improvements are still required. Mechanisation of handling dried filter press cake, as by means of fork lift trucks, may have made conditions worse rather than better; the increasing throughput of material sometimes with shift working has further aggravated the situation.

Measurements made in 1939 by the Thermal Precipitation[5] of respirable dust concentrations in the body powder preparation department handling dried filter press cake, gave results calcualted to be of the order of .8 mg/m^3. Recent determinations in a department carrying out similar processes with a Casella[6] sampler indicated concentrations of respirable dust of about 1.5 mg/m^3. While these results are clearly not representative of the whole industry, they confirm the wisdom of changing from filter press cake drying and grinding to other methods of preparation.

Reductions in general atmospheric pollution can only be achieved by either controlling or eliminating the sources giving rise to it. Where the sources are diverse and difficult to control by orthodox means, any significant improvement is likely to depend upon changes in process. In dust preparation the technique of spray drying, well known in other applications, is now being used by some wall tile manufacturers to convert body slip directly into spherical aggregations of dried material entirely within an enclosed system. This preparation technique when integrated with totally enclosed methods of conveying could lead to a high degree of operational safety. While some manufacturers are approaching this ideal it has not yet been fully achieved.

Dust Conveying

Manipulation of prepared body powder from the dust preparation department to the presses and between the various stages in its preparation gives rise to a number of primary sources of dust which could be adequately controlled by exhaust ventilation, but in addition there are many secondary dust sources which are very difficult to eliminate. A major cause of this secondary dust is spillage but the problem of preventing atmospheric dust arising from the manipulation of prepared body powder might also be aggravated by the general but slight reduction in moisture content.

Spillage from conveyors is unavoidable but with well constructed enclosures having integrated spillage collecting bins it can be collected for emptying by vacuum, (fig. 23) or in some instances it might be possible to arrange for dust spilled from the conveyor to be discharged directly into hoppers. As complete enclosure of the conveyor is necessary to prevent the spillage of dust, it might be preferable to make the enclosure into

Figure 24. *Spilled material at a tile press — ordinary lighting*

the conveyor itself such as by using air fluidisation or mechanical transfer, so eliminating the need for moving parts within the conveyor enclosure, which inevitably requires maintenance, and for which some form of opening would necessarily be provided. Although no such scheme is yet in use, investigations are in hand which could lead to a system of pneumatic conveyer being installed in two factories.

Dust Pressing

Fully automatic presses are becoming increasingly common. Some new models have been introduced by continental manufacturers and an enlarged version of the Collingham and Owen press has become available. Means of controlling the dust evolved at the tools of presses were developed by the B Ceram. RA and recommended to the industry in the First Report, but the system is by no means universally applied and it is not often appreciated that even where such a system of control is operating efficiently, it does not adequately control all

Figure 26. *Spillage containment at a C & O press*

Figure 25. *Dust rising from spillage at a tile press Tyndall beam lighting*

the dust generated through the operation of the press. In press shops it has become increasingly apparent that greater attention to secondary dust sources is required.

Fully automatic presses are invariably surrounded by spilled dust (figs. 24 & 25). As this spillage appears to be unavoidable, efforts might best be directed towards its containment and safe disposal. This simple approach has resulted in the production of an integrated scrap containment system (fig. 26) for the new 100 Collingham and Owen press providing for the collection of dust spilled from the press table into bins which can be emptied by vacuum[7]. This same scrap system has been applied to other sizes of the C & O press. A further modification is proposed to the base of the machine to prevent possible accumulations of spilled material beneath the framework and to facilitate cleaning, but in the meantime concrete plinths cast around the machine can achieve the same benefit.

Fully automatic presses have necessitated the mechanisation of tile delivery to the stacking point and these conveyors can themselves be sources of dust as material adhering to the surface of the conveyor belt is released as the belt passes over an end pulley (fig. 27). Mechanical fettling of tiles is normally accomplished by the provision of fixed scraper pads at the side of the tile conveyor and sometimes this fettling is done without efficient exhaust ventilation. Attempts are being made to enclose and exhaust existing tile conveyors from presses in such a way as to encourage the inward flow of air past the worker at the stacking point where dust is also released into the atmosphere. A new prototype conveyor feeding an automatic stacker machine has been designed to achieve complete enclosure and is now working. Such a conveyor could also incorporate suitable scrap bins to facilitate vacuum emptying and so prevent any possible spillage of material on the floor.

Firing and Glazing
Separation of individual tiles from bungs after biscuit firing can result in the evolution of atmospheric dust,

Figure 27. Dust released from a tile conveyor band as it passes round an end pulley — Tyndall beam lighting

but control by enclosure with exhaust should be possible. Other dust sources, such as those arising from the edge cleaning after glazing, also lack efficient exhaust draught in many instances, but this may well be regarded as less urgent than the dust sources within the press shop.

Production and Employment

In 1956 it was reported that 40 factories in North Staffs were engaged in tile manufacturing, employing a total of over 6,500 workers with a further 16 factories employing almost 2,000 workers in other parts of Great Britain. The estimated numbers of those factories and workers engaged in wall tile manufacturing are shown in table 19 together with equivalent numbers for 1970.

Of these 1970 totals, only eight factories in Great Britain employing less than 4,000 workers include biscuit tile manufacturing by dust pressing processes. Others are factories concerned only with glazing and decorating, or tile production using a different method. The number of workers estimated to be employed in various processes in wall tile manufacturing in 1956 and 1969 are given in table 20. The numbers employed in factories outside North Staffs are estimated only, whereas the figures for North Staffs are taken from census returns. Thus it is apparent from the totals for North Staffs that although the total number of workers employed in wall tile manufacturing has risen substantially, the number of workers engaged in the processes up to and including pressing has not shown the same proportions increase.

During this same period the output of glazed tiles has risen by a very much greater extent than the rest of the pottery industry. The output of glazed tiles in square yards expressed as an index (1949 = 100) rose to over 200 in 1966 and 1967, (Machin and Smyth, 1970) and from 1956 to 1967 the increase was nearly 50% (from index 133 to index 203). Thus the average increased output per tile worker during the period 1956 to 1967 was about 41% and the increase per person employed in pre-firing processes was slightly greater.

The rising rate of production per person is indicative of increasing mechanisation, especially in the dust pressing department. Although fewer dust preparation units are now in production, the high intensity of production has necessitated the employment of more workers, in some instances on an almost continuous shift basis.

The potential danger of increasing dust concentrations through mechanisation should be averted by the recent development and further applications of process enclosure.

Table 19. Factories and workers in wall tile manufacture 1956 and 1970

	1956		1970	
	Factories	Workers	Factories	Workers
a North Staffs.	16	3,289	11	3,680
b Rest of GB	6	900	6	1,990
Total	22	4,189	17	5,670

Sources:
a Census of employment and records of HMFI Stoke-on-Trent.
b Estimate based on Industrial Health Report (Ministry of Labour and National Service, 1959) and HMFI records.

Table 20. Distribution of workers in wall tile processes 1956 and 1969

	1956			1969		
	a North Staffs	b Rest of GB	All GB	c North Staffs	d Rest of GB	All GB
Sliphouse	86	25	111	74	22	96
Dust preparation	52	15	67	81	32	113
Pressing and Fettling	786	220	1,006	782	354	1,136
Decorating and Glazing & Glost Warehouse	2,365	640	3,005	1,138	410	1,548
Other				1,605	1,172*	2,777
Total	3,289	900	4,189	3,680	1,990	5,670

Source:
a & c Census of employment, HMFI Stoke-on-Trent 1956-1969
b Estimated total from the Industrial Health Report — distribution estimated from 1956 North Staffs. Census.
d Totals, Annual Reports of HM Chief Inspector of Factories. Distribution assumed to be similar to that in North Staffs.

*Includes nearly 500 workers in a factory making tiles other than by dust pressing.

Floor and fireplace tiles

The production of dust pressed floor tiles is now concentrated almost entirely into four North Staffs potteries employing about 500 workers. Fireplace tile manufacturing has also become concentrated and only three potteries continue production. These employ about 800 operatives.

The composition of the tiles varies considerably, from those made entirely from natural clays, such as the floor tile of the 'quarry' type to the vitrified tile, pressed from body compounds of white burning clays with silica additions. The total free silica content of floor and fireplace tiles is generally below that of glazed wall tiles, but where ground flint or sand is added, usually to vitreous bodies, the free silica content can be as high as 40%. The output of such tiles represents less than one quarter of the total volume of fireplace and floor tiles.

Prepared body dust for pressing these thicker floor and fireplace tiles requires slightly higher moisture content than is appropriate for thinner wall tiles. Thus not only is the number of employees at risk very much lower, but also the hazard would not normally be as great as in wall tile manufacture.

Of the total number of operatives in floor and fireplace tile manufacturing, only a proportion would be employed in potentially dusty work and only a fraction of these would have been exposed sufficiently long for any pneumoconiosis to develop, hence the number of employees among whom pneumoconiosis might possibly be diagnosed is comparatively small and possibly as few as 40 although the number in the past would undoubtedly have been higher.

The number of cases of pneumoconiosis attributable to floor and fireplace tile manufacturing is very small, although dust exposure in these branches of the industry may well have contributed to the pneumoconiosis among some workers where their exposure was mixed.

The number of cases and potential cases is too small to provide any basis for a comparison of hazard with other parts of the industry. The need for improvement in housekeeping and dust control is recognised and efforts are now being made to secure reductions in atmospheric dust concentrations by changing dust preparation techniques, possibly with co-operative body dust production, rather than applying 'first aid' measures to existing plant.

Recommendations

Efforts to reduce the free silica content of tile body powder should continue. Special care should be exercised to ensure that mechanisation and other process changes do not increase dust evolution, but rather changes should be exploited to prevent dust emissions. Continuing attention should be paid to secondary dust control, particularly spillage, floor cleaning and handling, and the aim should be to achieve as far as possible, production entirely within a closed circuit system.

Sanitary Whiteware Manufacturing

In 1961 the Joint Standing Committee issued a circular to all sanitary whiteware manufacturers making three recommendations on the basis of work carried out by the B Ceram. RA. These concerned the use of terylene overalls, exhaust ventilation for casting shops. These rates of general ventilation for casting shops. These recommendations were afterwards confirmed in the First Report.

A special survey was undertaken by the Secretary in 1967/68 to ascertain the extent to which the existing recommendations had been implemented, and if possible, to assess their effectiveness and relevance to the present methods of production. In addition to the basic study of the degree of acceptance of the earlier recommendations, attempts were made to estimate the possible effect of potential developments on the health of the workpeople. These related matters of special importance concerned changes in body composition and the development of new techniques which could both reduce the number of workers at risk and also reduce the concentration of the dust to which workers are exposed.

The survey raised a number of basic issues which, besides having special relevance to the sanitary whiteware industry, must also concern the whole ceramic industry. These include the need for greater emphasis on secondary dust, especially that arising from the floors, and progress already has been made in dealing with the joint problems of scrap control and floor cleaning.[8] The need for periodic review of the application of earlier recommendations on developing situations was also revealed.

Copies of the survey report were distributed to the manufacturers concerned and formed the basis of a series of consultations between HM Factory Inspectorate and the individual manufacturers as well as their trade association, the Council of British Ceramic Sanitaryware Manufacturers. The recommendations were accepted by the Joint Standing Committee and immediately distributed to the manufacturers as a guide for action. The remainder of this chapter is based on the Secretary's report.

Structure of the industry

The survey covered all 15 factories in which sanitary whiteware was produced. These factories were operated by 12 different companies linked into four main groups. Only six factories were in the Stoke-on-Trent Factory Inspectorate district with two others fairly close. These six factories employ about 30% of the total number of sanitary whiteware workers and about the same proportion of the casters. In 1959 there were 22 sanitary whiteware manufacturers in Great Britain of which eight, employing about 40% of the workers, were in the Stoke-on-Trent district. Since the survey the number of factories concerned has been further reduced but the number of Stoke-on-Trent workers engaged in sanitary whiteware manufacturing has increased. (table 21).

At the time of the survey 1,100 of the 3,620 employees in all GB sanitary whiteware factories were casters and a further 165 were regular casting shop workers. The majority of the 'other workers' were not engaged in particularly dusty operations.

Table 21. Numbers of operatives employed in sanitary whiteware manufacture

	1956	1959	1961	1963	1967	1969
Sanitary whiteware Workers (Stoke)	—	1,184	1,181	1,226	1,100	1,339
Sanitary casters (Stoke)	—	387	407	406	360	417
Total Pottery (Stoke)	48,200	45,200	43,000	41,000	38,100	38,339
Total Pottery Workers (GB)	62,500	58,900	58,400	56,800	54,000	51,900

Source:
Lines 1 & 2 Survey 1967-8
Line 3 — HM Factory Inspectorate, Stoke-on-Trent, employment census (see Part 2 — Structure of the Industry).
Line 4 — HM Chief Inspector of Factories. Annual Reports (Department of Employment, 1952-1970)

Dust Disease

The figures given in Table IV (ii) of the first report of the Joint Standing Committee suggested that sanitary casters were at substantially greater risk than most other workers in the pottery industry. However, the basis of comparison may not have been entirely satisfactory as other factors could have influenced the figures[9]. An examination of the figures for the five year period 1964 — 1968 reveals that the average years of exposure of workers before first assessment by the Pneumoconiosis Medical Panel varied from 20 for the milling industry to 40 in the china industry. The average period for the 18 cases among sanitary workers was 32 years. Cases attributed to mixed industrial exposure have not been included.

The distribution of these cases among the various sanitary production processes is shown in table 22 which clearly indicates the relatively high degree of risk for workers in casting shops.

The employment census for 1967 indicated that the 360 sanitary casters constituted 33% of the total labour force in sanitary whiteware manufacturing, (table 21) but casters contributed 72% of the pneumoconiosis assessments among the sanitary workers during the period 1964-68 (table 22). If the two potters' shop (mixed) cases were to be included with the sanitary casters, the proportion of the assessments attributed to casting shop workers would be 83% although they represent only 36% of the total labour force. All 18 cases concerned pre-fired processes in which about half the workers are engaged.

In 1964 several cases of pneumoconiosis were

Table 22. pneumoconiosis among Stoke on Trent sanitary workers 1964-68

Average exposure in years before first assessment

Casting	Occupations Other than Casting		
Casters 27 (13)	Placers	46	(2)
	Potters shop (mixed)	32	(2)
	Sliphouse	60	(1)
	Average	43	(5)
Overall average for sanitary workers		32	(18)

Source: Stoke-on-Trent Pneumoconiosis Medical Panel
Figures in brackets give the number of cases.

reported among glaze sprayers after relatively short duration exposures, but none of the assessments in 1964-68 involved workers in this process.

In the First Report the number of assessments to sanitary clay shop workers over an 11 year period was compared with the number of workers employed in the processes to give an incidence of 19% or almost 2% per annum. A similar calculation for the period 1964-68 yields an incidence of under 1%. While this figure indicates some improvement, other factors, especially labour turnover and the effect of the mass radiography surveys, could mask the result of improvement in working conditions in sanitary casting shops. Furthermore, the interval between first exposure and assessment requires that the present incidence relates to earlier rather than present conditions. However, the rate of improvement in sanitary whiteware manufacturing appears to be slower than the pottery industry as a whole. Over the 19 year period for which records are available, sanitary workers contribute 8% of the total assessments for pensions, whereas over the most recent five year period, 1964-68, the proportion was 12%.

Body Composition

During the past 10 years the change over from earthenware to vitreous china has been completed with consequential variation in body composition. This change is normally associated with the use of nepheline-syenite instead of felspar and often with the change from flint to uncalcined sand. Typical outline recipes are given in table 23.

As compared with the earlier earthenware body, there has been a slight reduction in total free silica content, although where stone continues in use, the free silica content is still about 40%. The slightly higher free silica in the present sand based body may be partly offset by the assumed greater biological activity of the cristobalite into which some of the flint is converted during calcination. The principal benefit in changing from flint to sand would be to raw material processors, who might then be able to achieve higher standards of operational safety[10].

Any benefit resulting from the substitution of flint by sand is to be welcomed. The real solution of the health problem will require a more far reaching change, namely the use of such fillers as will produce a body with an insignificant free silica content. It was reported that some such materials have been considered and extensive trials made, but the increase in cost which would result from their use as well as technical difficulties has been a major obstacle to progress. This difficulty may diminish if new techniques are introduced which actually depend upon bodies with low free silica content.

Dust sources

Dust is often considered as arising from two distinct sources, the specific dust sources specified in Regulation 17 of the Pottery (Health and Welfare) Special Regulations for which control by means of efficient exhaust draught is required, and other sources not so specified. The latter group of sources are normally grouped together and designated as the contributors to 'background' dust with the implication that they are naturally occurring and unavoidable.

The sources of dust in a sanitary casting shop, as in other pottery departments, are many and varied and often difficult to control, but attempts at identification followed by elimination or reduction might be practicable even where orthodox dust control methods are inappropriate.

In sanitary casting there is only one specific process prescribed in Regulation 17 as requiring exhaust ventilation, namely fettling other than damp fettling (which is defined) and little provision appears to have been made in dealing with other dust sources. These diverse sources of pollution are of increasing importance as the rate of throughput of material rises.

With the aid of a high intensity beam of light to supplement ordinary observation, a number of sources of dust have been identified, but more work is required to ensure that the list is complete. In some instances there are tried means of reduction if not elimination, but generally it seems that major changes in technique will be required to effect any substantial improvement.

Sanitary whiteware is produced by filling a plaster mould with a water suspension of prepared body which flocculates onto the mould and from which the water is absorbed by the plaster, leaving a cast which is subsequently dried, smoothed, glazed and fired. When a hollow cast is required the surplus body slip is tipped out of the mould after a sufficient layer of clay has formed.

As previously used mould sections are assembled for filling, dried scrap falls from the outside of the moulds on to the benches and floors and some of it becomes

Table 23. typical body recipes

Approximate percentage of ingredients

	Body A	Body B
Plastic base		
Ball clay	26	23
China clay	22	30
Flux		
Felspar	22	
Nepheline-syenite		15
Filler		
Flint	26	
Sand		32
Total free silica (estimated)	30	35

Figure 28. Spillage of clay along a casting bench after tipping

Figure 29. Trough for the return of tipped-off slip

airborne dust. This can be seen in a number of photographs, e.g. figs. 28 and 29. This scrap comes from the overflow of slip during filling, spillage when tipping out, and escape of slip at seams. It is aggravated by the irregularities in the moulds and the continued use of steel bands and wedges for mould assembly.

Elimination of this dust would depend on keeping clean the outsides of the moulds by the production of more accurate mating faces of mould section, with means of preventing the slip escaping at joints; and the provision of automatic filling and vacuum emptying or other means of emptying instead of tipping. The use of plastic funnels with washing after each time of use could also effect improvements.

Slip is spilled over benches as well as the outer surfaces of moulds during filling and attempts to catch poured-off slip in troughs or buckets when making hollow casts are never entirely successful. After pouring it is usual to see a pool of slip between each mould as well as spillage over the mould itself and over the benches (fig.28). Troughs, where used, are somewhat better than buckets (fig.29) but experience in china casting suggests that pipes would be preferable to troughs. The effective use of pipes may depend on the establishment of single mould tipping point, as might be possible with conveyorised production.

Vacuum or suction emptying, as practised overseas, is being tried but the drain casting process may be eliminated by the application of newer techniques such as pressure or automatic casting.

Figure 30. Partly opened moulds with scraps on the floor

Sometimes larger amounts of surplus clay have to be cut off, as at the top of the main section of a box rim closet. Containers for scrap are normally provided but much of the scrap is dropped on to the floor (fig.30). While improved methods of scrap collection are required,[11] immediate reductions in floor contamination would result if employees exercised greater care.

The mould is prepared for re-use by picking off some of the larger pieces of clay, especially on mating surfaces and sometimes by scraping spilled dried clay from the top of the mould. These clay fragments fall on to the floor to add to the scrap arising from spilled slip and plastic clay.

It is unlikely that any very substantial improvements could be made without a change in technique such as pressure or automatically controlled casting. However, conveyorised casting with a single mould stripping point would facilitate control of the scrap and dust by limiting the area in which it is generated.

A crucial stage of production follows the removal of the cast from the mould and preliminary cleaning — the process of drying the cast from about 19%-20% moisture to the 1% maximum before the ware can be fired. From each 30lbs cast, about one gallon of water has to be removed by evaporation either from the cast itself or from the mould. As this water evaporates the cast shrinks, and if drying is not uniform the variations in shrinkage would cause splitting and so spoil the ware. The danger of spoiling is greater where hollow sections of varying thickness with sharp angles go to make the cast. Insides of angles, particularly on the interior of the cast, will be the slowest to dry while outer surfaces, particularly at rims, will dry rapidly. In the sanitary industry the problem has been partially overcome by slow drying in the open workroom, with some general heating. Although this drying can take up to five days it may be accelerated without danger by using a coarser body which minimises the moisture content variation through the body of the material.

Drying is normally accelerated by means of ducted warm air or steam heating. Steam pipes beneath casting benches enable the caster to dry his moulds overnight, though sometimes drying is continued during the day. Casts are also dried mainly during the night by means of steam pipes or warm air ducted beneath the racks.

Drying is not in itself a source of dust but the handling of dry or semi-dry casts in the open workroom produces dust (figs. 31 and 32). This dust appears to be an inherent feature of the present production system and it may be that prevention will only be possible by a change to controlled drying in specially designed plant instead of in the open atmosphere of the workroom.

Figure 31. Dust rising from the handling of a 'green' fettled closet with about 13% moisture

Figure 32. Dust rising as a 'green' fettled closet is placed on a rack for drying

The day after casting, the cast is placed on a small turntable, (fig.33) set in a fixed or mobile bench, and the seams and rough patches removed by scraping. Tap and waste holes are cut out. After further drying, the cast is returned to the bench for 'looking over' which involves minor fettling of previously uncorrected faults and fettling of tap and waste holes etc. The ware is then taken out of the department.

When all fettling was done with the cast white-dry, so much dust was produced as to make the operation the greatest single dust source. This is no longer the case as most fettling is now done while the cast is still semi-damp. The change has reduced, but not eliminated the evolution of dust from the process.

Where quick drying bodies are used, the moisture can be as low as 13%-15% within a few hours of stripping, so enabling the bulk of the fettling to be done on the day of casting. After overnight drying, the moisture content may have fallen to about 7% or less so that any fettling undertaken the day after casting could produce substantial amounts of dust. With ordinary body compositions, most fettling is done the day after casting when the cast is still damp, but surface drying is so advanced that scraping produces some dust.

Casts made on Fridays are almost invariably left till Monday for fettling; although polythene sheets (themselves sources of dust when soiled with dry clay) are used to 'hold back' drying. At the time of the survey, white dry fettling was being done by casters in a number of sanitary whiteware factories each Monday. Dry fettling was also done by casters who had fallen behind with their work and in one factory it was found that casters were regulary fettling ware which had reached a state of white dryness after about five days.

In every factory it was possible to find white dry fettling operations, albeit minor ones, associated with 'looking over' regularly carried on by the caster himself in the casting shop. (fig.34).

Dust arising directly from the scraping of casts is very small when the moisture content is high, but the fragments of clay remaining on the surface of the ware dry very rapidly and atmospheric dust rises as the surface is subsequently disturbed by handling (fig.31). Fragments of moist clay from the fettling of 'green' casts also appear to dry when falling through the air, so that while the heavier particles fall to the bench or floor, smaller dust particles can remain airborne. The debris on the benches and floors also gives rise to atmospheric dust as it is disturbed after further drying.

It should be possible to reduce the amount of dust in the air of the casting shop by ensuring that no fettling is done in the casting shop other than sponging or cutting off seams after stripping the mould. This could be achieved by the removal of all casts from the shop on the day of making. Forced drying might then be desirable. All fettling operations which produce dust could then be carried out in suitable hoods which should both control the dust evolved during the process and eliminate, as far as practicable, the secondary dust sources.

The need for fettling might be very much reduced by careful design and manufacture of moulds, the use of improved mould clamping methods or the new technique of pressure casting.

It is usual to have separate inspectors to check each cast and make good the minor blemishes or return the cast to the casters for more substantial rectification work. Some white dry fettling is done and the B Ceram. R A type

Figure 33. Mobile fettling bench

Figure 34. Dust rising from minor fettling of dry castings

Figure 35. B Ceram. R A type fettling hood in use

exhaust hoods (fig.35) are normally provided. Where adhering dust is removed by compressed air jet, the efficacy of the exhaust hood is impaired. The air pressure and jet size should be controlled to give the minimum air velocity and volume. The possibility of removing dust while the ware passes along an enclosed and exhausted conveyor from the inspector to the glazing department should be explored.

Glaze is normally applied by spray, in one factory automatically, and in one small department of another factory by dipping. Dust arising from spraying is largely controlled by water-wash spray booths but significant escapes of dust can sometimes be detected when improved dust control is necessary.

Some ware is found to have blemishes after firing and most factories find it worth restoring this to first quality rather than let the work go as cheaper 'seconds'. Blemishes are polished off with abrasive hand tools or machines, and glaze re-applied to the faulty parts for refiring. The control of dust produced by polishing is not always satisfactory and some consideration is now being given to the use of low volume/high velocity exhaust systems (Department of Employment, 1970b) as the variation in shape and size of the ware makes the use of the orthodox type exhaust hood rather difficult. As the fired ware is non absorbent, artificial drying is sometimes provided. Leadless glazes are generally used although low solubility lead glazes are occasionally used for making good repairs.

Substantial amounts of clay scraps have to be returned for reprocessing and these scraps can give rise to dust. The sources of return scrap clay are:

a   Tipped off slip. When poured slip is collected in buckets it is frequently transferred into wheeled containers which are tipped into a slip chute for pumping back to the sliphouse. Wherever slip is poured from one container to another there is spillage and in all workrooms where buckets are used it is usual to find a bucket storage area where they are turned upside down to drain. Floors of these areas are heavily contaminated with scrap clay.

b   Plastic scrap from trimming. Shallow trays[12] (fig.50) are frequently used to contain this scrap but are quite unsuitable and of insufficient capacity. When full these trays weigh over ½ cwt. and could well give rise to strains as well as increasing the likelihood of scrap falling from them on to the floor. Some rare examples of more suitable scrap containers on wheels have been seen.

c   Floor scrapings etc. Scrap spillage on the floors is often scraped up during the day so giving rise to dust[13] (fig.48).

Figure 36. Dust rising from the movement of a caster's foot

There can be no doubt that more dust arises from the floor than any other single source. From early in the day, scrap falling to the floor adds to that remaining on the floor from the previous day; this dries and is trodden into dust by the feet of casters and other workers and by the wheels of any internal transport (fig.36). Scraps from fettling also fall to the floor and even where the B Ceram. R A type of bench is provided, this floor contamination is not entirely eliminated (fig. 35). The gross variations in the amount of scrap on the floor between different working positions indicate that some workers maintain higher standards of housekeeping than others, notwithstanding any present disadvantages or difficulties in the production system.

Terylene overalls are preferable to cotton or other materials on account of the reduction in airborne dust arising from the re-evolution of dust retained on the surface of the fabric. The dust frequently arises from the drying of adhering moist clay which is released by movement and carried into the breathing zone of the worker by convection currents. The difference between cotton and terylene is only relative and some dust is still released from the fabric. This is unavoidable but might possibly be reduced by personal de-dusting units which are used in some continental ceramic factories. Means of de-dusting overalls at frequent intervals, or more frequent laundering of overalls should be considered.

New developments

New developments in the industry are aimed primarily at cost reduction and fall into two categories — modification of existing techniques and the introduction of entirely new ones.

a   The modifications to existing techniques are mainly intended to improve productivity and involve degrees of mechanisation from the use of multiple filling heads on the slip pipe to fully automatic production units.

Developments appear to be entirely piecemeal but if the best features of individual experiments could be drawn together into a single joint development there is no doubt that a greatly improved system of production could be devised. Modifications so far in use or contemplated are:

Mould filling. Attempts are being made to automate the operation of feeding slip into moulds. Earlier efforts to control filling with a valve controlled by a photo electric cell were not pursued although its practicability is demonstrated by the successful introduction of this type of control in domestic earthenware production. This development could lead to a reduction in atmospheric dust rising from the handling of moulds by minimising the encrusted dried slip which often results from over filling.

Mould Emptying. The removal of slip from moulds by suction instead of tipping should be practicable and would also reduce contamination of the outside of the moulds. Automatic casting units in current use abroad utilise this method of mould emptying.

Drying. Sanitary ware could be dried quickly under controlled conditions if the techniques employed in the manufacture of large electric insulators were used. Here, the first stage of drying during which contraction occurs, is controlled by means of 'humidity drying'. This system consists of drying the ware in an enclosed atmosphere by raising the temperature and so maintaining a high degree of relative humidity. When most of the contracting has occurred and the danger of splitting averted, the dryer is ventilated and the drying process can continue with air changes until the moisture content is down to 1% or 2%. Mould drying is a straightforward process which could be done within an enclosure, but the need for this has not arisen and may only become important where two or more casts are required from the same set of moulds in a working day.

Conveyor Casting. By mounting the moulds on conveyors it should be possible to provide a single casting point, stripping bench, etc. The integration of this system with automatic filling, suction emptying, and conveyorised drying would undoubtedly make this idea much more feasible now than when the attempt was made over 30 years ago. If developed, this system would greatly facilitate the control of dust and could lead ultimately to the integration of casting, fettling, drying, glaze spraying and firing, possibly using a small cross section kiln or even a hover kiln of the type now being introduced into some other parts of the ceramic industry.

As a modification to the method of moving the moulds, it would be possible to have an automatic filling and emptying system moving past fixed moulds. After stripping, the casts could be taken directly by conveyor to a fettling hood and thence by conveyor to the other processes. Mechanised or automated units are successfully used in Europe to produce casts in the green state ready for fettling and glazing in the usual way. It is unlikely that the automatic units as used abroad could be introduced into British factories without a restriction in the variety of shapes, so making possible the large runs which would be necessary for such automatic plant to be economically efficient.

b New methods being contemplated involve the use of high density slip, plastic clay or dust. These methods are expected to greatly increase the rates of production and require less drying by evaporation, so effecting savings in fuel costs, etc., in addition to reducing labour charges and other overheads. Some of these new methods are:

Pressure casting. The major basic research at present being actively pursued is the casting of high density slip into reinforced moulds at high pressures, so producing what is virtually a filter press cake in the finished shape. The introduction of this process could result in substantial reductions in the concentrations of atmospheric dust: fewer moulds would be used and handled; the process could result in less spillage over moulds and benches and the floor, and the accurately made moulds could reduce the amount of fettling. As far as is known little emphasis has been placed on the health benefits which could be expected from such a development.

Dust pressing. As far as is known this technique is not applied to sanitary ware although some domestic tableware has been produced experimentally. The use of dust pressing methods for producing simple shapes is under consideration.

The American ceramic industry seems to be aiming at the use of prefired body constituents probably with no free silica which can be pressed into shapes with a suitable binder and then fired for a short time only. This technique enables pressed ware to be fired and finished on one day and would lend itself to conveyorised production as there would be no difficulty over drying. The spread of this idea to this country could lead to increased interest in dust pressing.

The extension of dust pressing techniques to the sanitary ware branch of the ceramic industry could be a retrograde step unless accompanied by a reduction in the free silica content. Wall tile manufacturing produces a higher incidence of pneumoconiosis than electrical ceramics. Although there is a slight difference in moisture content of the dust used for pressing, the most significant difference is the much lower free silica content in electrical ceramics.

It is understood that fast firing techniques will require the exclusion of free silica, thus any introduction of dust pressing associated with fast firing could bring substantial health benefits.

Plastic clay pressing. There is as yet little development in the pressing of plastic clay, a technique which is said to be used abroad for the production of difficult as well as simple shapes. This method of production might facilitate improved standards of housekeeping.

Previous recommendations

In 1957 the B Ceram. R A reported on the work to reduce the dust inhaled by casters in sanitary casting shops, the need for such work being long recognised. At that time the change to green fettling had not been long established and for many years white fettling had been acknowledged as the major source of respirable dust. It was shown that during the fettling operations, blowing clean, temperature-controlled air from a large orifice mounted above the operative would prevent dust rising into his breathing zone. This arrangement was designed to work with a positive means of general ventilation to prevent a build up of dust in the shop atmosphere. Although the arrangement brought improvement for the operative, it did not control the dust at source and so prevent it from entering the atmosphere of the workroom as required by Regulation (SI.65,1950).

Further work by the B Ceram. R A resulted in the development of the hood combining the experience of the earlier arrangements with the standard methods of dust control by enclosure and exhaust ventilation. It was intended that one hood should be provided for continuous use by a fettler serving several casters. This method of working was tried in a few factories but has now been abandoned. Some manufacturers are providing exhaust hoods for all fettling by installing one hood to be shared by a small group of casters. Workers' objections have influenced this lack of development.

In the course of its work on exhaust hoods, the B Ceram. R A found that much of the dust in the caster's breathing zone was given off by the overall. At that time they were made of cotton fabric which was found to have considerable dust retention properties. The testing of other materials led to the recommendation that terylene should be used for the overall supplied to casters in pursaunce of the Regulation. Simultaneously, work was carried on with mechanical ventilation to dilute the dust in the air of the workroom with air drawn from outside. This had been foreshadowed in the early attempts at feeding clean air to the caster. It was accepted that the number of casters rather than the size of the workroom was the important factor in dust concentration; 750 cfm per caster was suggested as the suitable air-inlet rate. On the basis of this work, the Joint Standing Committee issued a circular in 1961 recommending to the trade that:

a   exhaust ventilating hoods should be provided for all fettling which gives rise to dust

b   terylene overalls should be worn

c   dilution ventilation should be provided at a rate of 750 cfm/caster.

These recommendations were subsequently confirmed in the first report of the Joint Standing Committee for the Pottery Industry "Dust Control in Potteries".

In only two factories was there any attempt at division of labour to provide master fettling points, but the B Ceram. R A type hoods were normally provided for inspectors and often made available to casters doing white fettling. Some hoods with exhaust only were used and these were generally more popular than the combined blower/exhaust hood. Some firms have tried personal variations of the B Ceram. R A hood but so far none has been entirely satisfactory.

The use of terylene overalls is now almost universal, similar overalls also being supplied to other casting shop workers in most factories. There were a few complaints that they were uncomfortable but this was usually due to excessive workroom temperatures.   A small number of workers had produced certificates from their doctor claiming allergy.

The attempts at dilution ventilation were rarely related to basic principles. In only a few factories was the installation designed in accordance with the recommendations of the First Report, the usual faults being lack of mechanical assistance and permitting air to flow from the casting shops into other workrooms, or from other places where dust could be present, into the casting shop. Where a mechanical system of ventilation was provided it was frequently not used. Air changes and movement were often regarded as a production device for controlling temperature and thus the drying rates rather than for the dilution of atmospheric contamination.

The management often left the workers to decide for themselves whether to use the dilution ventilation system and sometimes it was found they preferred not to use it until the casting operation had been completed.

Table 24 indicates the extent of the provision of acceptable dilution ventilation, but does not reflect any failure to use it. Acceptance in the Stoke area is such that one third of casting shop workers are employed in satisfactorily ventilated workrooms and almost 50% in partially ventilated workrooms, depending on either natural inlets or outlets with inadequate mechanical assistance. In the case of 'out-potteries' 36% of the workers were employed where there was little or no dilution ventilation and only 17% worked in casting shops with a reasonably satisfactory ventilating system.

Table 24. Dilution ventilation

Number of employees in casting shops

	Stoke	Outside Stoke	Totals	% of casting shop workers
Recommended standard	135	150	285	22
Doubtful	185	415	600	50
Below recommended standard	70	315	385	28
Totals	390	880	1,270	100

Satisfactory has been taken to indicate conformity with the JSC recommendations and no extensive checks have been made to ensure that the end results of diluted contamination are achieved. Approximate determinations of atmospheric contamination suggest a slightly higher level of contamination in factories outside Stoke as compared with sanitary casting shops in Stoke-on-Trent where the rate of general ventilation is higher.

The principles of dilution ventilation which may require further examination or clarification appear to be:

a   That the incoming air is clean.

Reports of substantial levels of general atmospheric dust in the air outside factories in the Stoke-on-Trent area have not been confirmed but higher concentrations could occur in the vicinity of factories where the discharge of air from dust extraction plant is too low to achieve adequate dispersal. Better dispersal of dust discharged into the outside atmosphere would result from more careful siting of dust units. Not only should general low level discharge be avoided but special care exercised to ensure that there is no direct re-entry of dust from extraction plant into workrooms.

b   That the incoming air is thoroughly mixed with the dusty air and the flow so arranged that dust is not caused to become airborne.

Earlier work by the B Ceram. R A demonstrated the beneficial effect of arranging a downward air flow of fresh air past the workers but the original dilution ventilation systems often involved the introduction of warm air beneath racks — an arrangement more suited to ware drying than dust dilution. This practice has unfortunately been copied in some recent installations while some potters' shops incorporated air intakes and outlest at a high level, so ensuring a short circuit of clean air across the top of the workroom and giving little benefit to the workers.

It was frequently found that only an inlet or outlet was provided and some installations appeared to disturb dust from ledges etc. so aggravating rather than improving the dust problem. This adverse effect of dilution ventilation was probably the combined result of an excessive rate of air movement and inadequate cleaning of the workroom.

c   That clean air is supplied at the correct rate.

The rate at which air is supplied should be related to the concentration of respirable dust in the air of the workroom. It is first necessary to ensure that all sources of dust are controlled as far as possible so leaving the dilution ventilation to deal with those sources which are genuinely uncontrollable. The rate of 750 cubic feet of air per minute per caster was recommended when the throughput of clay was of the order of 80lbs/caster/hour. The present throughput of material, including scrap return has now greatly increased dust and the recommended rate of 750 cubic feet per minute/caster may need revision.

Conclusions and recommendations

Pneumoconiosis records indicate that sanitary casting shops have been hazardous and it seems that fundamental changes in materials or processes will be required to ensure complete safety.

In the long term the first emphasis should be on materials. The principle of substitution of safe for hazardous materials should be the aim. In practice this means using ingredients which give rise to a level of toxicity which can be tolerated without significant risk to health. It is conceivable that such a level could be set in terms of total free silica content below which the risk would be sufficiently low that no special precautions would be required by regulations, in addition to those imposed by the Factories Act on all dusty processes.

If materials used are hazardous when present in the atmosphere as airborne dust, the processes giving rise to the pollution must be so controlled as to prevent potentially harmful concentrations. This requires stringent controls over all aspects of processes which could cause atmospheric pollution and special attention to the problem when new techniques are being developed. While guards can be fitted to machines which have not been designed to perform with safety, it is often too late to impose efficient and economic health safeguards on a process which has not been designed to be accomplished without risk to health.

In dealing with existing problems the term

'background dust' should be avoided and the atmospheric pollution recognised as airborne dust arising from uncontrolled sources. The proper approach would be to identify all dust sources, eliminate them wherever possible and where practicable to control by exhaust ventilation those which remain. Dilution ventilation should be reserved for genuinely uncontrollable sources such as clothing. Exception could be made for 'minor sources' when they have been identified and assessed. The use of a monitoring device to determine the level of contamination for comparing with a threshold limit value is a useful check, but it must always be remembered that determination of dust concentration is no substitute for elimination or control, whatever the level of contamination may be.

The recommendations of the JSC in its first report dealt with the then existing problems of dust in sanitary whiteware manufacturing, and would now seem to require further consideration in their application to changing conditions.

Summary of recommendations

With regard to existing methods of production:
1   Efforts should be made to identify and eliminate, reduce or control all sources of atmospheric dust.
2   Modifications in methods of production should be sought such as to eliminate the deposition of materials on the floor.
3   The industry should examine its methods of production with regard to:
    (a) fettling by casters without local exhaust ventilation as required by Regulation 17(1) of the Pottery (Health and Welfare) Special Regulations 1950;
    (b) the failure to clean workbenches as required by Regulation 19(2) of the Pottery (Health and Welfare) Special Regulations 1950.
4   Floor cleaning methods should be examined.
5   Dilution ventilation should be recognised as a secondary safeguard, its principle clarified and correctly implemented. A good level of general ventilation is invariably necessary.
With regard to future developments:
Health should be a major concern in any change of:
(a) materials where free silica reduction should be a primary aim, and
(b) methods, where the aim should be to avoid the introduction of any new process and plant which results directly or indirectly in the pollution of the air of the workroom.

Domestic Ware Manufacturing

Two trends of fundamental change have been noted over the past ten years which could affect, for good or ill, the incidence of industrial disease; new body formulations have been evolved and mechanisation is advancing, sometimes accompanied by change in basic techniques. Both these changes could be exploited to improve conditions of work as well as bringing productivity benefits.

Body composition

As the free silica can be regarded as the principal hazardous ingredient in pottery body, any change in recipe should ideally seek to reduce the proportion of free silica and ultimately lead to its virtual elimination. One of the most notable changes in body composition within the last 15 years was the introduction of a new vitrified ware in which alumina was partially substituted for silica. Another vitrified body, English Translucent China, was introduced about ten years ago, and more recently, the successful use of alumina as a partial substitute for free silica in vitrified hotel ware has enabled the potential hazard of the material to be reduced and it is to be hoped that this same trend will now spread into the domestic tableware field.

Work on new earthenware and vitrified body formulations, possibly with calcined clay, magnesia or other synthetic materials to replace some or all of the free silica is progressing both in the laboratories of the B Ceram. R A, trade suppliers, and in individual factories. It is hoped that these efforts will lead to a substantial reduction in the amount of free silica and so further lessen the risk to the health of the workers.

An earlier attempt to use micro pulverised flint in earthenware manufacture has, fortunately, been abandoned as this trend would have increased the proportion of respirable free silica in the prepared body. Where free silica elimination or reduction cannot now be achieved, and where no further reduction in the proportion of respirable particles is at present possible, the material containing the free silica should be handled in the least hazardous form. The free silica content of bone china, about 10%, arises from the use of stone, hence any silica-free substitute would make possible the production of a bone china which could be considered intrinsically safe from the pneumoconiosis point of view, and so warrant less stringent precautions.

In the meantime it would be preferable for ground stone which contains substantial amounts of free silica to be obtained and used in slop form (Joint Standing Committee for the Pottery Industry, 1970b).

Figure 37. Integrated cup making machine

Production methods

No part of the industry has experienced more rapid change in the last decade than domestic ware production, although the degree of mechanisation may not yet equal that of tile manufacturing where automatic plant has long been in use.[14] The shaping of plastic clay for domestic products was revolutionised by the introduction in 1959 of the British invented heated roller for spreading clay on to plaster moulds. This technique, which has found rapid acceptance in British potteries and is now made under licence by foreign machinery manufacturers, provided a means of fully mechanising the basic shaping process and so has prepared the way for further mechanisation of related

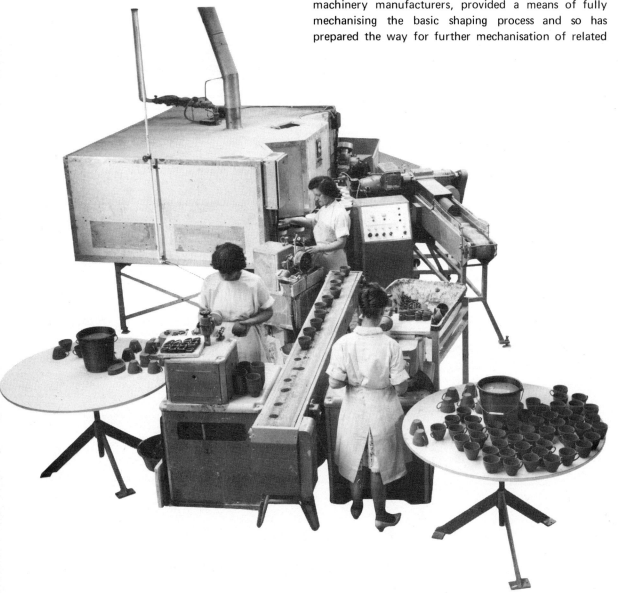

processes. The mineral oil (Joint Standing Committee for the Pottery Industry, 1969b) initially used to lubricate the shaping heads has now been replaced by oil which is either free from or has been specially treated to remove, possible carcinogenic agents. In this way vigilance has prevented the possible introduction of a new hazard into the pottery industry. Efforts are now being made to integrate separate mechanised units into fully automatic productive systems, some of which are now coming into use (fig.37). While this progress in mechanisation is well advanced in most factories and progressing towards automation, some manufacturers still depend largely on the hand work of craftsmen.

This progress has not involved the development of new techniques but rather the modification of old established methods. Attempts to press flat ware from prepared dust as in tile manufacturing have not been pursued. The longer term significance of these changes is not only that fewer persons will be at risk from any dust which could arise from a process, but also that a high standard of operational safety could be achieved by the application of closed circuit principles with efficient control of spillage and scrap return, and hence of potential secondary dust sources.[15]

Similar, but less radical benefits can be derived from the limited developments now being applied to a number of stages in domestic ware manufacturing. Sliphouse operations have become simplified but so far there are few examples of mechanised handling with automatically controlled blending. Attempts to mix dry ingredients with water in a pre-pug mixer have not been pursued, but this technique would almost certainly be capable of application if dried prepared body dust or granules were made available to the British industry. Any extension in the manipulation and use of dry prepared body with a substantial free silica content otherwise than in an entirely enclosed system would be regrettable.

While plastic clay shaping has advanced, casting processes are still generally undeveloped and are reported to cause more atmospheric dust than some other shaping methods. A few isolated attempts at mechanisation have brought some of the hoped-for improvements. The problem of dealing with scrap[16] scattered when handles are shaped by casting has to some extent been mitigated by improved designs of bench with integrated scrap control; but a more fundamental improvement could well result from

Figure 38. Dust released when handling dried flat ware

suitable mechanisation, possibly incorporating impact moulding machines to shape handles from plastic clay.*

Secondary shaping, particularly towing, has undergone important change. Improvements in mould design and making has made possible the elimination of face towing, while for edge smoothing, which is still necessary, several semi-automatic machines are available. An earlier semi-automatic machine provided with a hood of the type described in Appendix IIIA of the First Report was found to require modification to ensure an air flow across the ware being moved to and from the stacks on the feed and discharge tables of the machine where secondary dust was released (Appendix 4.1). This same release of dust into the atmosphere has been noted at another semi-automatic towing machine which had effective exhaust draught at the towing heads (fig. 38).

The recent introduction of wet smoothing machines to replace towing operations has eliminated the primary dust sources and so avoided the necessity for local exhaust ventilation. Some existing dry towing machines have been converted to wet sponging. Similarly wet sponging is replacing some of the fettling of cast ware. Where the control of primary dust from towing and fettling necessitated the provision of exhaust ventilation there was also at least partial control of any secondary dust. Means of dealing with these secondary dust-sources will have to be devised.

Handling of clay ware generally gives rise to dust and the problem is frequently aggravated by the use of foam plastic or similar padding on boards and trucks used for conveying dried clay ware (fig. 39). Cushioning materials which do not evolve dust, such as cellular rubber rings, should be substituted. As boards soiled with clay release dust into the air of the workroom when moved, more advanced methods of ware handling to eliminate these sources of dust would be preferable. In the meantime frequent washing, possibly by machine, would be advantageous.

Cup and other turning of semi-dried clay has in the past resulted in the distribution of clay fragments over a wide area of floor and bench. It was anticipated that mechanisation would bring a solution to the problem. The arrangements described in the First Report effectively controlled primary dust but did not adequately control the scrap which indirectly results in the evolution of dust into the atmosphere. The development of a pneumatic sequentially operated guard giving enclosure of the cutting head(fig. 40), together with integrated scrap collecting arrangements, was designed to meet the wishes of HM Factory Inspectorate and has produced further improvements.

* Cup handling machine made by Service Engineers Limited

The use of alumina for bedding bone china for biscuit firing, itself a substitute for flint, is now giving way to the use of profile refractory setters which are also being introduced into some earthenware factories where sand has been the traditional placing medium. Much of this sand is spilled and fragmented by traffic so adding to the hazardous dust which is released into the atmosphere by its manipulation especially after firing which converts at least some of the quartz into a possibly more hazardous form of silica.[17] (Department of Employment, 1970a). The design of rim nesting shapes has enabled many manufacturers to avoid the necessity for any support medium at all except when firing large and irregular shapes for which alumina or zircon sand might be a

Figure 39. Dust released from foam plastic cushioning

Figure 40. Improved dust hood at a cup turning machine

(See also appendix IIIC of the First Report)

suitable material where profile setters are not practicable.

Biscuit brushing by hand has been eliminated in a number of factories by the use of vibrating cleaning machines but local exhaust ventilation is required. This has been tested at some machines by the B Ceram. R A and found to control the dust satisfactorily. (Appendix 4.2)

The trend towards the greater use of lithographic transfers instead of hand application of colour for decorating ware has continued along with the mechanisation of making processes, and consequently the distribution of workers by occupation has remained reasonably constant. It is unlikely that any future diminution in the number of workers concerned with making will be matched by an equivalent reduction in those engaged in decorating. As no assessment for pneumoconiosis pension has been attributable to dust exposure in decorating departments the proportion of pottery workers potentially at risk should decrease with any further reduction in clay shop workers.

number of accidents have been directly attributable to the necessity for handling larger unit weights.[19]

Mould making, common throughout the industry but concentrated in tableware manufacturing, has traditionally depended upon the use of plaster but in recent years the introduction of metal spraying of cases and the use of resin based blocks has grown. Initially the metal used was a low melting point alloy containing lead but this has now been replaced by other non toxic metals. Resins, invariably epoxy, are possible causes of dermatitis and appropriate precautions should be taken where they are used, including the provision of adequate washing facilities close at hand, the use of barrier creams, adequate management supervision and, wherever possible, medical supervision. The use of silica flour as a filler should be avoided and less hazardous materials substituted. General advice on the use of these materials and the precautions to be observed was distributed to pottery manufacturers by the Joint Standing Committee for the Pottery Industry. (Joint Standing Committee for the Pottery Industry, 1968b).

Related hazards

Overalls of suitable design and fabric as recommended in the First Report are normally worn by operatives in clay shops in an endeavour to minimise secondary dust emission from clothing. The effectiveness of the overall is sometimes reduced by wearing other clothing outside. While the necessity for this practice can sometimes be averted by effective control of the temperature[18] operatives should be discouraged from wearing clothing outside overalls (JSC for the Pottery Industry, 1967c).

Burns from hydrofluoric acid are now very rare, largely the result of the introduction of substitutes for hydrofluoric acid which was previously used to clean unwanted decoration from finished ware. As the use of hydrofluoric acid for this purpose, as distinct from etching, had largely disappeared, the JSC recommended that the residual use of hydrofluoric acid for this purpose should cease completely. (Joint Standing Committee for the Pottery Industry, 1967a).

Bulk packaging of goods for despatch from potteries has largely ceased in favour of carton packing of sets of ware so eliminating much of the use of straw and with it also any possible hazard of 'farmer's lung' associated with exposure to dust arising from handling straw. Where filled cartons are themselves packed into cardboard cases the total weight of the final package can be sufficient to give rise to risk of injury and, in fact, a

Recommendations

Any change in body composition should be such as to reduce the respirable free silica content. Means should be sought to eliminate the use of free silica in subsidiary processes such as case making with resins or in the placing of earthenware for biscuit firing. Development in production techniques and raw material handling which eliminate dust sources, such as the use of ground stone in slop form instead of dried, should be encouraged. Special care should continue to be exercised to ensure that secondary dust sources are minimised, and when new machines are introduced adequate precautions against dust emission should be incorporated. As far as possible the aim should be to achieve production within an enclosed system.

Hydrofluoric acid should not be used for cleaning unwanted decoration from finished ware.

1, 2, 4, 9   Part 2 Dust Disease
3   Part 2 Structure of the Industry
5, 6   Part 4 Dust Measuring
7, 8, 11, 15, 16   Part 4 Scrap Control
8, 13   Part 4 Floor Cleaning
10, 17   Part 3 Flint Milling
12   Part 4 Scrap Clearing
13, 18   Part 4 Temperature Control
14   Part 3 Tile Manufacturing
19   Part 2 Accidents

Control
Measures

Secondary sources of dust have attracted increasing attention and some have been investigated with a view to securing their elimination or control and endeavours to improve the standard of dust control at specific primary sources have been continued. The results of these efforts are described in this part. An environmental factor relevant in attempts to reduce atmospheric dust is the 'corrected effective temperature' which combines temperature, humidity, radiant heat and air movement. Suitable target standards are recommended together with advice on attaining them. Instruments which enable dust concentrations to be monitored are described.

Scrap Control

Present methods of pottery manufacture utilise only a proportion, sometimes as low as 60%, of the clay delivered from the sliphouse to the making departments. That material which does not constitute the shaped ware is normally returned to the sliphouse for re-processing. The means of collection, conveying and return of this scrap into the production cycle do not receive the same consideration as the processing of the clay which continues on through the making cycle as shaped ware.

The cost of collecting, transporting and reprocessing the scrap is very substantial and is further increased by the subsequent cleaning of any spillage.

Methods of collecting scrap frequently rely on the use of shallow trays which, besides being difficult to handle, are neither suitable for mechanical handling nor minimising any release of dust into the workroom atmosphere. This problem was considered by the Technical Sub-Committee (Joint Standing Committee for the Pottery Industry 1969a) and provisional guidance given to some manufacturers. Some consequential developments are encouraging, especially the general appreciation that the problem requires a solution for reasons of efficiency as well as of health.

The elimination, or at least reduction of scrap should always be the first aim and may be attainable by modifying the making methods, but where this is not possible, attention should be paid to the containment of the scrap where it is generated; its collection into suitable containers such as to prevent spillage or release of dust; its transport to the body preparation department without spillage or re-handling, and its disposal either as waste or back into the making system in such a way that dust is not released. Wherever practicable all these aspects should be considered together in drawing up a comprehensive scheme for scrap handling.

Scrap from primary shaping

The introduction of large capacity shaping machines (fig.37) simplified the problem by concentrating scrap generation at a small number of fixed locations. Where such machines are combined with clay feed units metering exact quantities of plastic body to the making head, the amount of scrap is minimised. Complete containment of the scrap and its immediate return to the clay feed unit to be mixed with fresh body would provide a solution. This has in fact been done successfully in the case of one design of automatic cup machine (fig.41). Alternatively, a local scrap clay blunger designed to produce a controlled pint weight slip from scrap clay could serve one machine or a group of machines, returning the scrap to the body preparation as a slop. Two such blungers have been specially developed.*

Where a scrap disposal system cannot be intergrated with multiple small output units, careful design can ensure that scrap is collected into suitable containers. It is particularly important to match machines and containers to ensure complete collection, and the use of standard scrap containers as part of an integral material handling plant can assist. Size and frequency of emptying should be matched to the rate at which scrap is produced (fig.42).

*Edward & Jones Ltd. and Wm Boulton Ltd, Stoke-on-Trent.

Figure 41. Mechanised scrap collection and return the feed unit at a service automatic cup machine

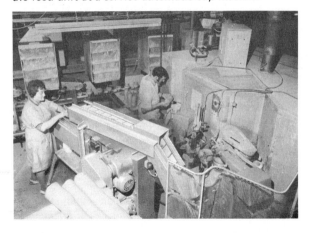

Figure 42. Overflowing scrap container at a new cup making machine

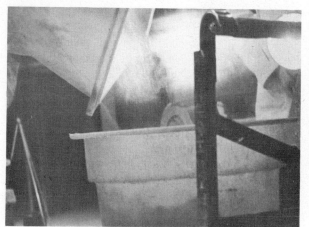

Figure 43. *Dust rising into the atmosphere as scrap is transferred from a collecting to a transporting container*

Figure 44. *Mechanised feed of scraps into a blunger with local exhaust ventilation to control any dust*

a Locating the scrap bin on the lifting device

b Tipping into the blunger

Ideally scrap should be transported in the container in which it is collected and not tipped into separate trucks or bins (fig.43).

Scrap containers should preferably be mounted on wheels or designed to be handled by a fork truck or tug lift device. Scrap should be tipped direct from the container into the blunger, or blunger feed unit, under the influence of exhaust draught, and never tipped onto the floor for subsequent shovelling into the blunger. While the blunger would normally be in, or adjacent to, the body preparation department, in many instances there might be advantage in providing local scrap blungers in strategic parts of the factory for piped return of the scrap to the body preparation department. Where it is not possible to instal the scrap blungers immediately below the tipping point, a dust free means of emptying scrap containers should be provided, e.g. totally enclosed inclined conveyor to the blunger from an exhausted tipping hood or a mechanical lifting device (fig.44).

The same system of scrap collection and return could be extended to match up with suitably modified benches where substantial quantities of scrap are produced, for example at cup handle fixing benches.

A long standing problem at dust presses[1] is the spillage of dust around the machines which is frequently recovered by shovelling. As this spillage cannot be prevented, containment and safe disposal is necessary. A modification of existing enclosure and scrap collection arrangements such as that made at certain tile presses can contain this spillage within the machine enclosure from which it can be emptied by means of piped vacuum system (fig.45). It is possible that the recovery of this spillage entirely within a closed circuit would enable uncontaminated material to be collected for re-use.

Casting is one of the shaping processes producing large quantities of uncontrolled scrap mainly as a result of fragments falling off encrusted moulds, spillage of slip when filling and tipping and cutting surplus clay from the semi-dry castings. Tipping at a fixed point and the use of vacuum emptying might reduce spillage and facilitate piped return. In the long term, however, any radical improvement is more likely to result from process changes. In one factory considerable improvement was made by mounting the casting bench over a series of hoppers designed to gather scrap into suitable containers, whilst at another bench, a rail-mounted container is used to collect poured off slip which is pumped to an adjacent blunger.

Secondary shaping

Fettling, towing and other secondary shaping processes generate relatively little scrap, but it is more hazardous on account of the low moisture content. The fact that the quantity involved is rarely worth processing has led some manufacturers to collect this material in disposable plastic containers (fig.46). By these means scrap can be collected under the influence of exhaust ventilation and sealed in impervious containers for safe disposal. This development of scrap handling can be applied to towing and fettling hoods of the type described in Appendices III A & B of the First Report. Alternatively a fixed container of the type provided at the new tile presses could be incorporated for emptying by vacuum.

Handling and inspection of shaped clay ware produces scrap which is often thrown towards, but not always into, the shallow trays which are usually provided. One tableware manufacturer has provided numerous reject and scrap collection tables which are emptied into suitable mobile bins by patrolling quality control inspectors who are thereby enabled to maintain an adequate check on reasons for rejection and so take early remedial action. Not only has this improved the scrap handling but it has also reduced the loss rate.

Scrap bins for clay ware should form part of the comprehensive scrap collection and disposal system as used throughout the pottery, but where scraps are dry enough to produce dust, suitable lids should be provided on scrap bins. The provision of swing top bins designed for domestic use, brought unexpected improvements through the deliberate placing of scraps rather than casually throwing then in the general direction of a shallow tray.

Flatware is frequently shaped by spreading plastic clay over a mould so designed that during drying the surplus edge of dry clay, 'bittings', shrink and separate from the plate. These 'bittings' of dry dusty clay fall from the mould when the ware is gathered for towing. In the case of dobbin dryers these 'bittings' are scattered on the floor at the working position and inadequate space beneath the bottom shelf normally precludes the use of other than shallow containers. The working level and construction of the take-off at mangle dryers has enabled some manufacturers to provide scrap hoppers to deliver the 'bittings' into containers but satisfactory arrangements for collecting this scrap at dryers are rarely possible. In some factories the problem has been eliminated by the design of moulds which do not produce 'bittings' and it is hoped that this practice will become more common.

Where the system of production has been so modified as to minimise the amount of scrap produced and provision is made to collect and reprocess these scraps without producing dust, the effectiveness of the arrangements will still depend upon the use made of them by the employees. It is essential that all employees should minimise spillage and dispersal of scraps and so conduct their work as to safeguard their own health and that of their fellow workers.

Figure 45
Emptying a scrap
container integral
with the dust
control hood
at a tile press

Figure 46
Modified hollow-
ware fettling hood
with plastic bag
container for
disposal of scraps

Recommendations

New production systems and machines should be so devised as to incorporate effective means of intercepting scrap and returning it for re-processing without releasing dust into the atmosphere or scraps into the working vicinity. Existing machines and processes should be examined and modified wherever practicable to eliminate or reduce the production of scrap and to ensure that such scraps as are unavoidably generated are efficiently contained, collected and re-processed with the minimum of release of dust or material. To this end a comprehensive and integrated system should be provided wherever possible based on a local blunger for conversion of the scrap into a slip for piped return to the body processing department. Where local slip conversion is not practicable, purpose designed containers should be provided for handling and transport and tipped directly into the scrap blunger. Where loading into the blunger is mechanised, the opportunity should be taken to provide local exhaust ventilation. Improved bins, such as the swing lid type, should be used for the scrap resulting from hand operations.

All employees should co-operate in measures designed to reduce or control scrap or the dust arising from its manipulation.

Floor Cleaning

This chapter is based on joint investigations of HM Factory Inspectorate and the North Staffs. Polytechnic.

Dust rising from floors has long been recognised as a major source of atmospheric dust in pottery workrooms (National Council of the Pottery Industry, 1933). Earlier Regulations (Statutory Rules and Orders 1913, 1932) concerning the construction and cleaning of floors were amplified and reinforced Reg. 18 of the 1950 Regulations (SI 65, 1950) but the problem of dust rising from floors is far from being solved.

Scrap material dries readily when spilled on the floor and is subsequently disintegrated and disturbed by passing traffic to raise dust into the atmosphere. When the current regulations were made such traffic was predominantly that of workers but it now includes trucks, of which some are mechanically powered, dealing with a greater throughput of work, which in turn increases both the amount of floor contamination and

its rate of disturbance. Thus the floor of a typical pottery workroom, whether used for plastic clay shaping, casting or dust pressing has some dry impacted material and a general layer of loose dust.

The investigations into cleaning floors as prescribed in the 1950 regulations (Evans & Finikin in preparation) confirm the need for changes in established practices.

Principles of floor cleaning

The most effective means of preventing dust arising from floors is to eliminate the spillage and this is considered in detail under Scrap Control, page 63. Means of cleaning will still be required to deal with minor accidental spillage which is unavoidable. The essential features of any method of cleaning are:

1. the cleaning process should thoroughly clean the floor and not only remove a proportion of the contamination.
2. the cleaning operation should not itself be the cause of dust rising into the atmosphere, and
3. the cleaning should be carried out before the spilled material can give rise to dust.

This last criterion, which applies principally to gangways and working aisles, concerns not only the method of cleaning but, more directly, timing and organisation. Where spillage can be neither eliminated nor intercepted, the ideal would be immediate removal from any place where passing traffic would be liable to cause dust to rise into the atmosphere.

Earlier attempts to approach this standard by means of gridded floors were not successful although the dust enclosure which was recently designed for a tile press has been provided with a gridded floor to facilitate maintenance and tool setting without spilled material being trodden out over the floor of the workroom. Immediate removal of spillage was achieved by continuously washing the floor at a point where spillage from a mechanised casting system could not be prevented. This technique however is not generally applicable and some interval between spillage and cleaning is unavoidable.

The present practice of cleaning at the end of the day lies at the other extreme, ensuring the maximum accumulation of floor contamination and thus maximum atmospheric pollution. The cycle of cleaning should be designed to reduce the period between spillage and removal, especially in gangways or working aisles where traffic is expected, but if this is to go on during working hours then it is especially important that the method must be one which does not increase atmospheric contamination.

Figure 47. Dust released with the discharged air at a vacuum cleaning machine

Established methods of cleaning

The layer of loose dust can be largely removed by traditional methods but the impacted material adhering to the floor still remains and so may be loosened by subsequent traffic. This impacted clay can normally be cleaned only after abrasion.

In the course of the recent investigation, the effect of various cleaning methods on the floor of a sanitary casting shop having a loading of up to 30 lbs of clay residues per 100 sq. ft. was examined. Sanitary casting probably causes the heaviest floor contamination although casting shop floors are generally more heavily contaminated than other making departments. Vacuum pick-up was found to remove about 75% of these residues and the pick-up itself was found to release very little dust in to the atmosphere. Self-contained vacuum cleaners permitted substantial quantities of dust to escape into the air of the workroom unless high efficiency secondary filters were incorporated (fig. 47). Some machines tested discharged the air at such a high velocity that dust was likely to be raised from benches and ledges in the vicinity.

Although no more efficient than mobile vacuum cleaners, a central vacuum cleaning system with piped connections would enable the filtered air to be discharged externally. Such system is also useful for keeping ledges and plant free from dust which may have settled out.

The removal of clay scraps from gangways, as is required to be done between 12 noon and 2 pm. in an effort to reduce the accumulation of floor contamination during the day, is of limited benefit and has itself been found to raise dust into the atmosphere (fig. 48).

Sweeping 'by a moist method' at the end of each day, which generally supplements the midday dry scraping, is designed to ensure that floors are efficiently cleaned

Figure 48. Dust rising as clay scraps are scraped together

without raising dust. In a sanitary casting shop sweeping with damp sawdust was found to remove only 50% of the clay residues. While it is likely that the use of damp material when sweeping could in fact reduce dust, the token sprinkling of damp sawdust is certainly inefficient, the more so if it is spread over a large area in advance of sweeping (fig. 49). Further atmospheric dust rises from the disposal of material removed from the floor by scraping or sweeping (fig. 50).

The most effective of the examined methods of cleaning was swilling, using brooms to release the impacted clay. Although this method of cleaning was not wholly dust free, it was more satisfactory in this respect than sweeping 'by a moist method'. Tyndall beam lighting revealed that the mere flow of water across a dusty floor was sufficient to raise dust.

Floor cleaning by swilling depends upon the conversion of the solid residues into slip and subsequent rinsing with clean water. The removal of the liberal quantities of water which are necessary can often be facilitated by the use of machines to pick up surface water, so reducing the amount of drying by evaporation. Impervious floor surfaces would also prevent water absorption and minimise the rise in humidity as the floor dries.

Alternative cleaning methods

Scrubbing machines, some having self-contained reservoirs from which water is fed to the brushes convert the solid material into a thick slurry which must be removed. Unless rinsed into a drain, solid residues will remain after drying although they can be minimised by efficient removal of the slurry.

Mobile vacuum cleaners are now available to pick up the slurry produced by swilling or wet brushing of the floor, so leaving an almost dry surface from which residual moisture can quickly evaporate to give a clean dry surface.

Both scrubbing and wet pick-up machines are liable to release dust into the atmosphere. The scrubbing machines normally have flat rotating disc pads or brushes which generate a vigorous tangential air move-

Figure 49. Dust raised by sweeping with damp sawdust

Figure 50. Dust rising as sweepings are collected

Figure 51. Dust raised by the brushes of a floor scrubbing machine

ment which raises dust (fig. 51). The provision of a suitable skirt around the scrubbing head was found to reduce this tendency. The mobile vacuum cleaners, even when picking up wet material, were found to discharge dust with the filtered air unless high efficiency secondary filters were provided (fig. 47).

When scrubbing and drying machines are used separately the scrubbed area is often walked over before drying, so reducing the effectiveness of the cleaning operation. Combining the two operations into a single machine eliminates this difficulty and enables one person to work alone. A number of self propelled

machines of this type were tested and found to be effective in cleaning the floor. Although mains powered machines were the most compact, in practice battery powered machines were more convenient as they obviated the necessity for trailing leads.

The two battery machines tested had power capacity for about four hours continuous operation, but higher capacity batteries are available to enable each machine to be used for a full working shift before recharging. One of the machines had a convenient built-in charging unit so enabling the machine to be plugged into any mains outlet.

Figure 52. *Dust rising from the operation after combined scrubbing with pick-up machine*

Figure 53. *Flexible vacuum pick-up added to a floor cleaning machine*

As initially tested, one of these machines was found to release large quantities of dust in the discharged air but this was eliminated by the provision of a supplementary filter, which is now available to existing machine users. Despite the provision of a skirt, some dust was raised by the rotary scrubbing action (fig. 52). The other battery powered machine (fig. 53) was provided with a supplementary filter and employed a cylindrical brush which enabled clay lumps to be collected in a separate container, so reducing the likelihood of clogging the vacuum pick-up head and at the same time reducing the pint weight of the slurry. The use of cylindrical brushes also avoids the outward flow of air usually found at disc scrubbers.

These machines were not only effective in cleaning but may also be suitable for use during working hours, so enabling the frequency of cleaning, particularly along gangways and working aisles, to be increased with a consequential reduction in the cumulative levels of contamination.

The machines tested were not suitable for use in a cul de sac from which they had to be backed out, as in such circumstances the fixed vacuum pick-up did not completely cover the area traversed by the water spray and scrubbing head. Prototype modifications have been made to one machine to enable a flexible hose to be connected into the vacuum pick-up to facilitate the removal of slurry in such places (fig. 53).

The other difficulty, the inability to clean under benches and plant, is more serious and might also be partly overcome by using the flexible hose. The real answer might lie in the integration of building and plant design and layout to prevent possible accumulation of scrap in areas which are not accessible to the machine. While this solution might be principally applicable to new developments the use of cantilevered benches or the elimination of some of the legs and low level cross ties and enclosure around machines and plant positioned on a coved plinth, would greatly facilitate cleaning by machine in existing potteries. Wherever possible floor obstruction should be removed such as by the repositioning of pumps and ancillary equipment to wall brackets or raised pedestals.

Floor surfaces

Rough concrete or indented bitumastic flooring make cleaning difficult, whereas smooth surfaces were thought to increase the risk of accident through slipping. Non slip tiles are being used experimentally and if effective would have the additional advantage of being non-porous. Alternatively, pvc, which can be seam welded to form an unbroken impervious barrier over the floor surface, made cleaning easier and satisfactorily withstood wear during the short period of the test. Other means of treating floors to render them impervious or coatings to provide a smooth impervious surface with good wearing qualities are now available and might facilitate both cleaning and minimise water absorption.

Current legal requirements

The basic requirement of the complicated Regulation 18 (SI 65,1950) for floor cleaning in potteries is that floors should be thoroughly cleaned by prescribed methods. Two of those prescribed, namely 'cleaning by a moist method' and 'vacuum cleaning' do not achieve the basic objective of 'thorough cleaning'. The fact that in potters' shops this daily cleaning has to be supplemented by weekly 'washing or mopping with water' and that in those areas where there is a lead or a particularly high dust risk 'daily washing or swilling' is required, is an implicit recognition of this very fact.

Furthermore the restriction of the removal of clay scraps and even cleaning by a moist method to times when few workers are likely to be present also gives implied acknowledgement that those operations raise dust into the air.

While 20 years ago these detailed provisions represented an appreciable advance over previous practice, they were necessarily circumscribed by the state of knowledge and technical resources available at that time. It seems clear, however, from the most recent investigation that some of the methods specified in, or permitted by, the regulations fail to meet the three basic criteria set out in page 66.

By contrast the newly developed combined scrubbing and wet vacuum machines, while better satisfying these criteria, do not (because they combine a moist method with a vacuum system) fit easily into the current legal framework. In the case of potters' shops, the regulations require either cleaning by a moist method after the end of the day's work supplemented by weekly washing, or vacuum cleaning which may be carried out during working hours. These machines are, however, particularly well suited to continuous use throughout the working day and should, as explained above, preferably be used in this way, so avoiding the need for dry removal of scrap during the day. Substantial improvements in the standards of floor cleanliness have been reported by potteries using these machines.

The present regulations were framed at a time when the only alternative to hand cleaning was the use of vacuum and are so worded as to apparently preclude the use of wet scrubbing machines as an alternative to the specified methods of wet sawdust with weekly swilling or vacuum cleaning. It is important that the application of improved cleaning methods subsequently developed should not be deterred by legal difficulties; and manufacturers wishing to make the fullest use of such equipment may apply to the Chief Inspector of Factories for exemption from certain of the specified requirements of the present Regulations.

Recommendations

Pottery manufacture should be so arranged by management, and the work so conducted by operatives, as to minimise the spillage of material on floors, especially in gangways or working aisles.

Methods of cleaning floors should be such as to remove thoroughly the material which would otherwise give rise to dust without themselves contributing significantly to the atmospheric dust concentration. Whenever practicable, cleaning should be by swilling or machine scrubbing with water. Cleaning should be completed as soon as possible after the material is spilled on the floor and in any case not later than the interval at the end of the shift.

New factories should be so designed and constructed that floors can be swilled or wet scrubbed daily and floors of existing factories should be modified wherever possible to facilitate cleaning. In particular, workroom layout and plant arrangements should be planned to provide the maximum unrestricted floor area for ease and efficiency of cleaning.

In any revision of the regulations, opportunities should be taken to clarify the requirements relating to floor cleaning and to enable developments in floor cleaning techniques to be applied more readily to pottery workrooms.

Temperature Control

Many years ago workrooms of potteries in North Staffs were described as being, with very few exceptions, 'low, damp, close, small, dark, hot, dirty, ill ventilated or unwholesome'. Although many of 'these disadvantages' have now been successfully eliminated and conditions greatly improved, the problem of controlling temperatures and ensuring adequate ventilation has revived through technical changes especially those resulting in the introduction of heated plant into workrooms.

In the search for a solution the JSC set up a panel of engineers[2] first to define the problem and then to make recommendations. The report of the work of the panel dealing principally with excessive temperatures was presented to the JSC in September 1967 and duplicated for distribution to the Industry. (Joint Standing Committee for the Pottery Industry (1967b).

This section of part 4 is based upon the earlier report of the panel of engineers with additions to cover the related problems of winter heating.

A bi-product of human activity is heat, and the body can only continue to function satisfactorily if this heat energy is given off. The degree of balance between the rate of heat generation and its dissipation determines the subjective feeling of comfort. The rate at which heat is produced varies with the level of activity and from one individual to another but can range from 390 Btu/hr when resting, to 1500 Btu/hr when engaged in heavy work. (Institute of Heating and Ventilating Engineers, 1965). As this heat generation is unavoidable the feeling of comfort can only be influenced by controlling the factors governing the rate at which the heat is dissipated. These factors, which relate to the different methods by which the body loses heat, include:

Air temperature
Cooling by convection is possible if the air temperature is lower than the body temperature; the closer these become the less effective the means of cooling.

Temperature of surroundings
If surrounding objects are below the body temperature, heat can be given off by radiation, but hot surfaces would cause further heating of the body by radiating heat to it.

Humidity
A natural body cooling mechanism is the operation of sweat glands which effect cooling by causing the body to give up latent heat of evaporation. this method of cooling is more effective in conditions of low humidity but is obstructed by clothing particularly when made of non-absorbing fabrics.

Air movement
Continuous removal of the hot moist air enveloping a worker and its replacement by cool dry air increases the effectiveness of natural cooling by both convection and evaporation. Excessive air movement can result in discomfort through excessive heat loss.

A measure of the environment, taking account of these factors so as to give an indication of the level of comfort is given by the Corrected Effective Temperature.* (Bedford, 1940). This scale permits the determination of a value of the CET from a knowledge of the globe and wet bulb temperatures and the velocity of the air movement. A general range of CETs for Britain has been recommended. As many pottery workers are accustomed to working in higher temperatures than those found in industry generally, slightly higher temperatures might be preferable. For example, except for those engaged in heavier types of work, pottery workers would prefer a Corrected Effective Temperature within the range of 18°C-22°C (65°F to 71°F) rather than the recommended winter comfort zone of 15°C-19.5°C (59°F-67°F). (Institute of Heating and Ventilating Engineers, 1965).

Conditions in potteries

In an industry using a process depending upon heat drying and high temperature firing it is not surprising that temperature control problems should exist. Indeed, the average workroom temperature appears to have been rising in recent years. Visits made to a number of potteries confirmed that high temperatures were common, principally in making shops, dipping shops and in areas close to kilns. Differences as high as 17°C (30°F) between the outside shade temperature and the workroom were found in a few cases, although the more usual temperature differential was between 6°C (10°F) and 11°C (20°F). In the older potteries, the problem was aggravated by low head room. In modern pottery buildings, roof lights often permitted substantial solar heating, and the use of large workrooms permitted the heat from dryers and kilns to spread over a larger area than would have been possible in the small rooms of older buildings.

Movement of the air within the workroom was generally insufficient. Provided other factors influencing the corrected effective temperature are satisfactorily controlled, the ideal rate of air movement would be about 30 fpm (Fox, 1965) which is just perceptible. A workroom with an air movement of less than 20 fpm

---

* CET provides an environmental comfort scale of measure which combines all the factors affecting the sensation of warmth.

would usually be regarded as airless while 100 fpm would be considered very draughty.

The introduction of fresh air for the purpose of ventilation was also inadequate in both old and new buildings because dependence was commonly placed upon natural air flow. In some cases improvements had been achieved by the provision of mechanical extraction ventilation and in a few instances by means of plenum systems of air inlets.

The increasing use of dryers for removing moisture from shaped clay ware and glaze, removal of solvent from decoration and from some of the processes in the preparation of raw materials has contributed to the increased temperatures in many making shops. Examples of conditions found at three different operating positions near dryers are given in columns a, b and c of table 25, which also gives the corresponding outside shade temperature at the same time. The high dry bulb temperatures recorded indicated substantial heat additions to the atmosphere of the workroom. The amount by which the globe thermometer readings exceeded the dry bulb temperatures gives an indication of the amount of radiant heat which increased the corrected effective temperature. No substantial air movement, which would have reduced the CET was recorded, consequently the CETs given in table 21 are based on an air speed of 20 fpm, which is the minimum for this purpose. The humidity recorded was within the expected range for the season of the year.

Columns d and e give examples of conditions in a pottery where steps had been taken to minimise excessive temperatures. Although substantial improvement had been achieved, the CET in one instance was still above the published summer comfort zone of $17°C-22°C$ ($62°F-71°F$). The figures recorded in a more acceptable working environment are given in column f.

The replacement of the bottle kilns, which were mainly separated from the production workshops, by modern intermittent or continuous kilns sited entirely within the main pottery building, was also a substantial cause of increased temperature. Where the new kilns were situated below the production workshops, substantial amounts of heat were transmitted to the workroom above by conduction through the floor and also by convection through stairwells or other openings.

Legal requirements

The principal legal requirements are contained in Sections 3 and 4 of the Factories Act 1961 and Regulations

Table 25. Observed conditions at working positions near dryers

	a	b	c	d	e	f
Dry bulb temperature (°F)	75	84	82	75.5	73	70
Wet bulb temperature (°F)	65	68	67	63.5	62	59
Globe thermometer temperature (°F)	85	93	90	78	73	69
Corrected effective temperature (°F)	76	79	78	72	69	66
Relative humidity (%)	59	44	46	51	54	50
External shade temperature (°F)	61	63	63	63	63	—

15 and 16 of the Pottery (Health & Welfare) Special Regulations 1950 (Statutory Instrument 65, 1950). Regulation 15 sets out requirements concerning ventilation and Regulation 16 concerning temperature, but neither of these regulations prejudices the general provisions of Sections 3 and 4 which require ventilation by the circulation of fresh air and the maintaining of a reasonable temperature. These legal requirements generally concern dry bulb temperatures and take no direct account of radiant heat and air movement. It should be noted that Regulation 15 and Section 4 require not simply general ventilation but also that the ventilation should, so far as practicable, be capable of rendering harmless all fume, dust and other impurities generated in the course of process or work. In assessing the amount of ventilation required by law, that needed to replace vitiated air must be added to that necessary adequately to dilute dust or fume. Another practical requirement is that the amount of ventilation should be adequate to remove the excess heat losses occurring within the workroom so that the ambient temperature is controlled to comply with Section 3 and Regulation 16.

The maximum and minimum dry bulb temperatures are set by Regulation 16 and Section 4. The general requirement that a reasonable temperature should be maintained is supplemented by the specific restriction of a minimum temperature of $55°F$ ($12.8°C$) in workrooms where pottery is made by the compression of clay dust or is fettled, and $60°F$ ($15.6°C$) in workrooms in which a substantial proportion of the work is done sitting and does not involve serious physical effort. Although high temperatures are more frequently the cause of complaint that low ones, as means of restricting excessive temperatures are successfully applied, so the importance of recognising minimum temperatures will grow. Regulation 16(1) prescribes a maximum permissible temperature within the workroom of $75°F$ ($24°C$)

or 10°F (5.6°C) above the outside shade temperature whenever this latter temperature exceeds 65°F (18.3°C). This regulation is one of prime importance for it establishes the maximum permissible summertime temperature difference between the inside and the outside temperature of 10°F (5.6°C) which is a key factor in designing systems of temperature control.

Dryers

The simplest form of dryer is the enclosed box, either with racks on which the ware is placed on boards or into which trolleys of ware are wheeled, the enclosure being vented to the outside either by natural or mechanical means. Somewhat more sophisticated forms of dryers are those with rotating mould or ware carriers mounted on a vertical axis which, when rotated by hand, pass the ware through the heated zone of the dryer. These dryers normally have recirculating air heating systems, drawing air out of the dryer through a heat exchanger and then returning it to the drying chamber, a proportion of the moisture laden air being discharged to the outside atmosphere. The most common dryer of this type is the 'dobbin' (fig. 54) which is used for drying clay ware, although similar types are used by dippers (fig. 55) for drying glaze and by handle-makers (fig. 56) for drying moulds. A variation of the 'dobbin' dryer is the jet dryer which has air passages incorporated in the hollow shelves with apertures to permit the hot air to pass over the ware being dried. Seals are provided within the dryer to prevent hot air passing into the shelves when they are at the loading and unloading positions.

A further common type of dryer is the mangle (fig. 57) consisting of a rectangular tower from 10 to 30 feet in height, within which is a swing-tray conveyor. The ware is placed on the conveyor trays and passed through the heated zone and is dried before being removed. In some instances the dryer is extended into an inverted 'L' or 'T' section. A newer form of conveyor dryer within a horizontal tunnel (fig. 58) is now growing in popularity and is frequently integrated into mechanical production units. (See also fig. 37).

Steam is still frequently used to heat the recirculating air at dryers either by passing it through an external heat exchanger or, as in some mangle and other simple type dryers, by placing pipes within the dryer itself. Gas, now increasingly common, is almost invariably used by the provision of an external burner injecting the products of combustion and associated heated air into the dryer air input. Some dryers, particularly the newer tunnel types integrated with modern clay shaping machines, use

Figure 54. Dobbin dryer

Figure 55. Dipper's dryer

Figure 56. Handle casting dryer

Figure 57. Mangle dryer

Figure 58. Tunnel dryer

electrical energy by infra-red or radio frequency radiations. Operating temperatures very widely, from less than 39°C (100°F) to almost 269°C (500°F), the most common range being 49°C (120°F) to 82°C (180°F). Excessively high temperatures near dryers were caused by convected and radiated heat from the dryer and associated plant and by the escape of hot air from the interior. Although in many cases the problem arose from the design of the plant, poor installation, unsuitable methods of use and inadequate maintenance, often aggravated the conditions.

Prevention of convection and radiant heat losses

As the rate of heat loss from heated plant is related to the surface temperature, the most obvious method of minimising heat losses is to reduce this surface temperature by providing insulation. This insulation can be applied to either side of the hot surface but on existing plant is invariably applied to the outside. On new plant, insulation can be applied internally or, as is now increasingly common, packed into the cavity created by double skin construction. In one instance, where a dryer was intended for use in a confined space, cooling water was circulated through the dryer casing.

Calculations have shown that an average size 'dobbin' dryer with steam heating, working for about 3,000 hours per year could lose heat to the value of £60 to £80 if no insulation were provided. If such a dryer were supplied with steam through uninsulated pipes, as is sometimes the case, the total loss could well rise to more than £100 per annum.

The standard of insulation of dryers was generally unsatisfactory. Inadequate insulation of older dryer cases commonly resulted in external surface temperatures in excess of 32°(90°F). In a few instances, particularly with handle casters' dryers, the whole of the dryer case was a single thickness sheet metal construction without insulation. Improved standards of insulation at some newer dryers with considerably increased operating temperatures had reduced the surface temperatures to below those found at older plant. Exhaust and recirculation air ducts, heat exchange units and fan cases were often of uninsulated single thickness sheet metal and in consequence the temperatures of these parts was almost the same as the drying temperatures being used.

The range of thermal insulating materials used in the past is considerable and included such varied materials as asbestos in many different forms, magnesium carbonate, glass, cork, rubber and a variety of plastic materials. In general, all thermal insulating materials depend upon trapped air or gas for their effectiveness and indeed air itself in a sealed space may be quite effective.

The selection of the correct thermal insulation will be governed mainly by the temperature of the surface to be insulated. As the thermal conductivity of many materials increases with temperature, calculations should always be based on the appropriate operating temperatures and the comparisons of materials should always be made at those temperatures. The conductivity of some insulating materials also increases with moisture content. In potteries it is desirable that hygroscopic material be protected against the ingress of moisture.

The majority of thermal insulation materials are mechanically weak and should be protected from damage. Some form of surface treatment is also desirable in potteries so that the surfaces can be kept clean and free from dust. The use of sheet metal is superior to most other forms of surface protection but care must be taken to avoid the formation of thermal bridges across the insulating material. There are many materials other than metal that can be used to provide external protection, and the choice of which to use is dependent to a large extent on the situation, e.g. a duct at a height above the ground could adequately be protected by wire netting and a hard setting compound whilst the lower half of a dryer case in a position where it is likely to be struck by passing trucks would probably require substantial metal protection.

In selecting an insulating material, regard should also be paid to any hazards which may arise from its use. Generally, insulation materials are not readily flammable, but some may propagate flame and it is recommended that these should not be used. Conversion of dryers from steam to direct flame heating could increase the fire risk. Some materials suitable for application to steam dryers could be hazardous when exposed to means of ignition in converted dryers, especially when impregnated · with oil from ware shaped on roller making machines. Possible fire risk of insulation coverings must also be considered, for example, bituminous compounds, impregnated cloth tapes and scrim cloth which are combustible are commonly used as coverings. The dust arising from the application or removal of thermal insulation materials may also be dangerous, particularly if asbestos is used. Materials with a toxic hazard should be avoided and effective precautions taken to protect workers removing old insulation which may contain toxic materials.

An example of an insulated tunnel dryer is shown in fig. 59. The body of the dryer has been covered with an insulating board and the associated ducts with glass fibre protected with a hard setting compound. A newly built dipper's dryer, was also effectively insulated by filling

Figure 59. Insulated tunnel dryer

the cavity in the hollow sheet metal construction with glass fibre.

Radiant heat emission is also dependent upon the surface temperature and so will be reduced by effective insulation. Further reduction can be achieved by interposing between the heat source and the workroom a reflecting screen such as bright metal foil, metallic paint or sheet aluminium. Dark or matt surface finishes should be avoided as these substantially increase the rate of heat emission by radiation.

Much of the radiant heat to which the pottery worker is exposed comes from the shelves and moulds in the open section of the dryer and in many instances it is practicable to decrease the size of these openings. Perhaps the most outstanding example of the size reduction of feed and delivery openings is that on the dryers attached to automatic cup making machines shown in figs 60 and 61, where each opening is only of sufficient size to permit the passage of one mould.

Figure 61. Feed opening at a 'Service' dryer integrated with a cup making plant

Prevention of hot air emission

The escape of hot air from simple dryers of the box or mangle type without air recirculatory systems can be prevented by effective ventilation. Natural ventilation is not satisfactory. The siting of the outlets of the vent ducts, variation in external temperature conditions and unfavourable winds can all serve to negate the effectiveness of natural ventilation and reversed air flow can be induced by dust control or other air extraction plant in the workroom. The provision of a fan in the exhaust ventilation duct of a dryer ensures a constant flow of air through the dryer and an inward flow at the feed and delivery openings, beside providing better control of ware drying. Outlets of vent ducts should be carefully sited to avoid return of the expelled hot and dusty air into the workroom. Generally the discharge should be above the level of the eaves. It is important to ensure that adequate provision is made for the introduction of fresh air into the workroom to compensate for that drawn out through dryers and any other air extraction plant.

Air circulatory systems of dryers are normally so designed that the drying section is kept under positive pressure. Any leakage past faulty seals or poorly maintained partitions will necessarily be toward the workroom so giving an outward flow of hot air at operating openings. If the escape of hot air from such dryers is to be prevented, the direction of this air flow must be reversed. Some types of existing dryers can be modified to achieve this mode of operation.

Figure 62. Modified jet dryer

Figure 65. Air circuits giving negative air pressure in the drying chamber.

(a)   No separate exhaust fan

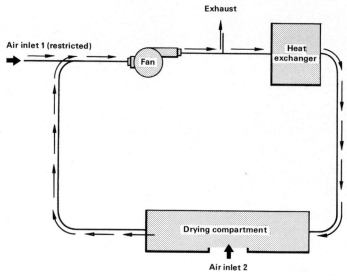

Figure 63. Modified dobbin dryer

(b)   Separate exhaust fan

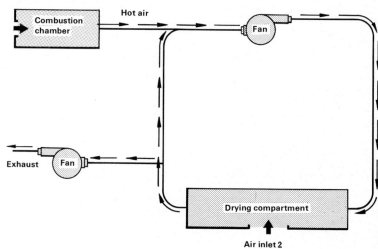

A suitable re-arrangement of the air flow system as applied to a jet dryer is illustrated in fig. 62. In this modification, ventilation extraction ducts have been fitted on each side of the opening. On the one side the duct returns air through the heat exchanger into the drying section, while the duct on the right side provides mechanical ventilation so removing from the dryer the bulk of the moisture given off in the initial drying stage. This ensures an inward air flow over the dryer opening.

Where re-arrangement of the internal air flow is not possible, the escaping air can be intercepted where it leaves the dryer and so prevented from entering the air of the workroom. This is illustrated in the dobbin dryer modification shown in fig. 63. A vertical extraction duct has been provided on each side of the operating openings and additional extraction is provided across the top. These extraction ducts are connected to the outside atmosphere by a vertical duct having within it an axial flow fan.

A variation of this type of modification is shown in fig. 64 where the working opening has been reduced from two to one segment and mechanical extraction ventilation provided above the one open segment.

The same technique of intercepting an outward flow of hot air has been applied to dippers' dryers but even where mechanical ventilation has been provided, difficulties have been encountered in capturing the peripheral air flow round the inside of the casing. It is also difficult to prevent the outward flow of air at handle casters' dryers. Sliding doors on the feed and discharge openings are only effective if they are kept closed. One modified handle casters' dryer, fig. 56, had interlock switches fitted so that the air re-circulating fan stopped when either door was opened.

Modifications to existing dryers to prevent the escape of hot air are generally only required because of incorrect initial design. Such design errors should be avoided in new dryers by designing the air circulatory system so that a negative static pressure is maintained in the dryer compartment. Fig. 65a illustrates a possible arrangement which will achieve this provided that

(a)   the back pressure of the exhaust system is always less than the air flow resistance of the heat exchanger and

(b)   that the fresh air inlet is restricted to provide only a fraction of the required replacement air, so ensuring that the remaining make-up air enters the system through the dryer feed and discharge openings.

If these conditions are not satisfied, mechanical exhaust arrangements would be required. This modification is illustrated in fig. 65b which shows a gas heated dryer which, like those using oil and waste heat, introduces the major part of the fresh air requirements into the hot air inlet by means of the re-circulating fan. The use of natural ventilation at such a type of dryer would result in a pressurised drying compartment and consequential escape of hot air through the feed and discharge openings.

Total reliance should not be placed on the existence of a negative static pressure to ensure an inward air flow into the dryer compartment. Consideration should also be given to the direction and velocity of the air flow at the feed and delivery openings to ensure that their velocities and directions are such that hot air cannot escape.

Substantial emission of hot air has been caused by unauthorised interference with the damper controls on the air flow ducts of dryers. All dampers or other controls which regulate the air flow at dryers should be so set that they do not permit hot air to escape from the dryer, and it is recommended that they should be locked in position to prevent unauthorised alteration. As an alternative to dampers the air flow can be controlled by orifice plates which are not susceptible to interference.

Figure 64
Modified dobbin dryer with a reduced opening

Kilns

If excessive temperatures near kilns are to be avoided it is important that heat released by convection and radiation should be contained and removed from the workroom and the means for doing this should be an integral part of the kiln installation.

Convection heat rising from the sides of kilns can be effectively controlled by fitting vertical insulation panels parallel to the sides with an air gap between the kiln and the panel, and with openings at the top and the bottom to permit the formation of a convection current through the air gap. If combined with a suitable hood over the kiln, the heat taken up by the convection current as it passes through the air gap can be conducted directly to the outside (fig. 66).

When a kiln is to be sited in a factory having parallel bays of roof trusses, the roof structure can be utilised as a natural canopy by positioning the kiln along a single bay rather than transversely across several bays. This arrangement will minimise the spread of the hot air rising from the kiln and facilitate a simple form of ventilation to remove the heat from the building. The effectiveness of this arrangement can be improved by suspending a continuous skirt as low as possible along the trough on each side of the bay and, if necessary, providing an enclosure across the bay a short distance from each end of the kiln.

Suspended skirt plates or a full canopy could be used when the roof or ceiling is flat. If a workroom is situated above the kiln thermal insulation might be required to reduce the heat conducted through the floor.

Table 26. Effect of radiant heat screens at an earthenware biscuit kiln

	Without Screen °F	With Screen °F
	a	b
Dry bulb	73	71
Wet bulb	62	65
Globe temperature	91	74
Effective temperature	69	69
Corrected effective temperature	77	70

The heat contained within such canopies is best removed by a mechanical extraction ventilation system so designed that the air flows in towards the kiln and out above it. This arrangement, if properly implemented, would prevent the spread of hot air to other parts of the premises.

In some instances hot air rising from the kiln contained flue gases because separate ducting to atmosphere was not provided. It is recommended that all flues and any opening directly into the ware firing chamber should be connected by suitable ducting to the outside atmosphere.

Radiant heat from kilns can also be reduced by the provision of side screens along the kiln and these can either be integrated with or separated from the thermal insulation provided to control convected heat loss. The effect of providing a corrugated aluminium screen fixed about 18 inches from the side of the kiln as illustrated in

Figure 66. Canopy over kilns

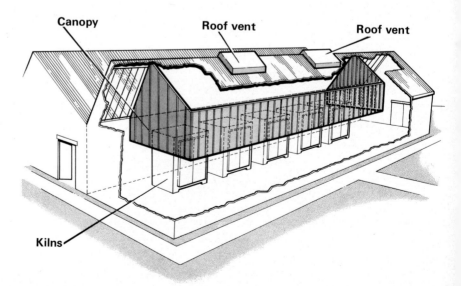

Canopy Roof vent Roof vent

Kilns

fig. 67 is demonstrated by the figures in table 26. The temperature measurements without the heat shield given in column A were repeated the following day when the screen was in position, column B. The radiant heat was so controlled as to reduce the corrected effective temperature to within the accepted summer comfort zone. Any trend towards smaller kilns close to operatives' working positions would require better control of heat emission, particularly radiated heat.

Recently fired kiln cars and the ware and kiln furniture upon them also contribute considerably to high temperatures, especially when trucks are removed prematurely from any cooling section of the kiln. When ware is passed through a kiln faster than originally intended the fired ware is inevitably withdrawn at a higher temperature unless the cooling capacity is correspondingly increased. Where such extension is not possible an effective supplementary cooling system is required to conduct the convected heat from the ware and truck to the outside and to shield against radiant heat emission. The air flow in such cooling tunnels or truck parking areas if (enclosure is not provided) should preferably be horizontal across the shelves of the truck as illustrated in fig. 68. Alternatively a cooling tunnel (fig. 69), also constituting a radiant heat shield, could be constructed with forced ventilation to take the convection heat outside the factory building. The amount of heat contained in recently fired kiln trucks might be reduced by the use of lightweight refractory blocks of low thermal capacity. This would not only minimise heat emission but would also attract the additional benefit of minor savings in fuel.

Figure 68. Kiln truck cooling by air extraction

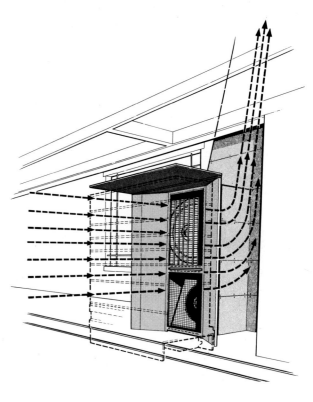

Figure 67. Radiant heat shield at a kiln

Figure 69. Kiln truck cooling tunnel

Control of general atmospheric temperatures

The main problem in potteries, unlike most other factories, is not winter heating but summer cooling to dissipate the substantial amounts of heat arising from the process. Even when heat losses from plant are minimised by the application of the measures described, it has been found that excessive summer temperatures can still occur if the residual heat losses from kilns and dryers, together with heat emitted from other sources, are not dissipated.

In order to determine the amount of heat to be removed in summer or added in winter it is necessary to draw up a 'heat balance sheet' (table 27). In such a balance sheet the estimated heat losses from the building, assuming internal temperature conditions to be within the comfort zone are set down against the estimated heat gains from the plant etc. and the difference gives an indication of the amount of extra heating or cooling required.

Solar radiation can supply substantial amounts of heat in the summer. Insulation of the building reduces this heat gain and it is recommended that new roof lights and windows should be so sited and constructed that they receive the minimum of direct solar radiation, and that suitable shading be provided for existing lights which are exposed to the sun. This same insulation would also serve to minimise the imbalance between heat gains and losses and so reduce the requirements for winter heating where required.

If, when reduced to the minimum, the heat gains are still the greater, the amount of general ventilation should be increased according to the formula.

Additional ventilation required =

$$\frac{\text{excess of heat gains over heat losses in Btu/hr}}{1.20 \times (t_1 - t_0)} \, ft^3/min$$

where t_1 is the inside air temperature and t_0 is the incoming air temperature (degrees F).

From trial calculations it appears that only in exceptional cases will it be possible to achieve the required additional ventilation by natural means, and that in the majority of cases a mechanically assisted ventilation system will be necessary. Such systems have an additional advantage in that they can be more easily controlled. In a few instances it has been found that the heat gain is so great as to justify the use of air cooling to reduce the temperature of the incoming air. It is preferable to supply slightly more air than the sum total of that removed from the room by the general and local exhaust ventilation systems, so maintaining the room under a slight pressure and preventing draught and the ingress of dirt. This additional ventilation might also serve to dilute any pollution of the air in the factory.

The source of ventilating air must be carefully selected, for instance, not close to a dust collector or from over a large area of potentially hot roof. In some areas the provision of air cleaning, cooling, or refrigeration may also have to be considered. The discharge within the workroom should be sufficiently diffused not to cause draughts (fig. 70).

In winter the air required to replace that lost through ventilation and dust extraction systems must be heated before feeding it into the air of the workroom. This heating can be achieved by means of recently developed gas fired burners which discharge the products of combustion into the incoming air flow. This system affords a convenient method of supplying the variable amount of heat necessary to warm a constant rate air flow to a temperature suitable for the workroom. The direct fired heating unit is satisfactory when all the air intake is from the outside of the building and precautions are taken to prevent any recirculation.

Additional heat input to compensate for that lost through the structure of a building could be supplied by introducing air at a high temperature, but in practice it is unlikely that a discharge temperature in excess of about $54°C$ ($130°F$) could be tolerated, at which level direct gas firing with no recirculation would not be expected to lead to high concentrations of the products of combustion. This additional heating may also be supplied by indirect means such as steam or electric radiators or by recirculating the workroom air through a gas or oil fired heat exchanger having a separate flue for combustion gases but a proportion of fresh air should always be introduced with the recirculating air.

Table 27. Heat balance sheet

Heat Gains	Heat Losses
From heated plant (dryers, kilns, steam pipes etc.)	Through structure — roof, wall, ceiling, floor.
From recently fired kiln trucks, ware and kiln furniture, and recently dried moulds and work.	Through windows and roof lights. By ventilation — Through dryers and kilns.
From equipment and machinery (electric motors and lighting)	Through exhaust ventilation system for dust control.
From personnel	General ventilation
From solar radiation.	

Figure 70. Inlet air diffuser

Waste heat, as from kilns, might sometimes be recovered for winter heating but a properly designed heat exchanger should be used to ensure that none of the fume or products or combustion from the kiln enter the air of the workroom. No attempt should be made to heat workrooms by the removal of insulation from heated plant during winter as this leads to uncontrolled and variable temperatures through the workroom.

Recommendations

Workroom temperature

As a design criterion, the heating and ventilating systems of potteries should provide conditions which fall within the range $18°C - 22°C$ ($65°F - 71°F$) 'corrected effective temperature'. This scale should be used in preference to the dry bulb temperature scale

Adequate ventilation to ensure that dissipation of any excess heat, and means of heating to compensate for excessive heat losses should be provided in all potteries.

Satisfactory means of control should be provided and used to maintain a reasonable temperature at all times.

In new building or reconstruction of existing potteries, expert advice should be obtained at an early stage to ensure an overall approach to the problem of achieving and maintaining satisfactory temperatures and special attention should be given to the process which is proposed or may be undertaken in the building.

Dryers

Steam pipes to and from dryers should be insulated to the economic thickness as determined by reference to the relevant British Standard, (British Standard Institution 1963, 1964), and all dryers and ducts, fans and heat exchange units used in connection with them should be so insulated that the general external surface temperature does not exceed $32°C$ ($90°F$).

The outer surface of thermal insulation should be finished so as to give mechanical protection and to permit cleaning.

No thermal insulation materials nor protective finish which readily propagate flame should be used.

Non-toxic material should be used wherever possible, but if thermal insulation materials containing asbestos or other toxic hazard are used, effective precautions should be taken to protect the workers involved in their application and removal.

All dryers and associated equipment should be so designed, installed, worked and maintained as to prevent the escape of hot air into the atmosphere of the workroom.

The feed and delivery openings of all dryers should be kept as small as practicable.

A positive inward air flow should be maintained over all feed and delivery openings of dryers during operation.

The outlets of the vent ducts should be so sited as to ensure that hot air cannot return to the workroom.

All dampers or other controls which regulate the air flow at dryers should be set to prevent the escape of hot air from the dryer, and when set they should not be capable of unauthorised alteration.

Kilns

Kilns should be so designed, constructed and sited as to minimise the likelihood of heat spread to other parts of the premises.

Suitable hoods and screens should be provided where necessary to control the heat lost from kilns and such ventilation provided as to ensure that the heat is extracted from the building. Kiln flues should be connected by suitable ducting to the outside.

Parking areas for recently fired kiln cars should be suitably screened and ventilated so as to ensure that the heat lost does not spread to other parts of the pottery.

Dust Control

The design of effective control devices for specific dust generating operations has continued. Since the First Report was published the development of suitable dust control apparatus for semi-automatic towing machines, improved cup turning machines and vibro-energy mills has been completed. These devices are described in part 3 and Appendix 4.

Following the practice of the First Report, dust control measures incorporated into machine design or in the form of a hood for a particular operation have been tested in order to establish the required air volume extraction rate and to determine the lower limit of air velocity at a test position. It is necessary that details of air extraction requirements and the minimum air velocity for efficient operation should be provided with the dust control apparatus.

Electro ceramic fettling

Investigations into the control of dust from the fettling of dust pressed electrical porcelain ware revealed problems peculiar to the industry which prevented the effective use of the fettling hoods previously devised for tile and domestic ware manufacturing These problems arose from:

(a) the large variety in the shape and size of ware of which some was too large to fit into existing hoods;

(b) the fact that not all fettling was performed while the work was held in the hand, but 'spotting', the fettling of holes or edges with a hand tool while the work rested on a board, was also common, and

(c) the need to control dust generated by cleaning the board. The method of working from a full to an empty board often resulted in a cleared board being cleaned of debris by knocking it on the floor at the side of the workbench.

Some manufacturers, recognising that the difficulties were aggravated by the methods of working, sought the help of works study engineers to guide changes, especially in handling methods and the length of ware-carrying board and thereby simplified the application of efficient dust control and at the same time improved productivity.

A variety of existing dust control arrangements and new devices specially developed to meet the particular requirements of electro ceramic fettling were tested under factory conditions to determine their effectiveness. Four of the arrangements which were found to give satisfactory control of the dust were described in a report distributed to the electrical porcelain industry. (Joint Standing Committee for the Pottery Industry 1968a).

The first alternative described in the report, was subsequently modified to accommodate shorter ware carrying boards which enabled dust to be efficiently controlled with a reduced extraction volume. The modified hood, fig. 71, has a sliding front panel so enabling the size of the working aperture to be adjusted. With an extraction rate of 1,000 cfm, dust was efficiently controlled with a front opening adjusted to 12¾ inches giving an air velocity of 160 fpm over the face of the opening and a horizontal air velocity of 140 fpm at a test point 6 inches vertically above the centre front edge of the lip with the ware board in position, or 170 fpm without a ware board. A red warning light has been fitted to give a clear warning to supervision when the screen is adjusted to give a front opening of more than 12¾ inches. An internal strip light is provided to facilitate inspection of the ware and to prevent irritating reflection of stray light in the front screen.

Arrangements have been made for scrap to be collected in a polythene container under the influence of exhaust draught so that the bag can be sealed for disposal of the waste. A bucket support for sponging is also provided.

In one installation two hoods of this type have been positioned back to back against an air extraction and filter unit so making a self contained unit with two working positions.

Figure 71. Fettling hood for electro ceramics

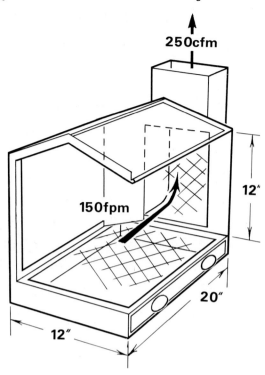

Figure 72. Modified hollow-ware fettling hood

250cfm

150fpm

12″

20″

12″

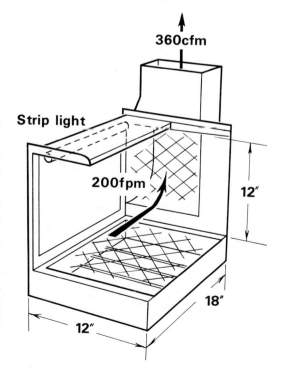

Figure 73. Modified tile fettling hood

360cfm

Strip light

200fpm

12″

18″

12″

A scaled down version of the hollow-ware fettling hood (fig. 72) described in appendix IIIB of the First Report, with side exhaust designed on the principle of tunnel air flow, has been found effective for the control of dust when fettling electrical porcelain. The sloping top and the rear vertical panels are of plate glass. The front of the hood and the left-hand side is open to permit pressings to be conveyed into and out of the hood by the operator's left hand. The base of the hood is formed by a shallow drawer 12 inches x 20 inches and the height of the front opening is 12 inches. The exhaust opening is on the right and the air is drawn across the front of the operative's body which forms the front side of the tunnel. As an alternative to the scrap drawer which should preferably be emptied by vacuum, it would be possible to provide plastic bags or other improved scrap containers. When tested by the B Ceram. R A, the horizontal air velocity at the centre of the hood was 150 fpm which is the minimum recommended. The volume of air necessary to achieve this rate of air flow was 250 cfm.

The tile fettling hood, appendix IIID of the First Report has also been found effective for electrical porcelain manufacture with the minor modification of covering only half of the top with plate glass. (fig. 73). The base of the hood is formed by a shallow tray 12 inches x 18 inches and the height from the top of the tray to the glass top is 12 inches. A strip light was fitted along the inside, rear, top corner. During the B Ceram. R A tests the horizontal air velocity at the centre of the hood was set at 200 fpm which is the minimum recommended for this hood. The volume of air exhausted was about 360 cfm. As in the case of the modified hollow-ware fettling hood various scrap collection arrangements are possible.

Another hood, fig. 74, designed especially for electrical porcelain fettling when using boards of 2 feet 6 inches In length encloses the entire bench except for the front working opening which can be varied by an adjustable glass screen. The front of the bench is formed by the gridded top of a scrap tray which could also be replaced by a plastic bag or scrap container for vacuum emptying. A strip light was provided to facilitate inspection. Air was extracted through the bench grid and at the back of the hood, and at the time of the test by HM Chemical Inspector of Factories the air velocity at the front of the hood was 150-200 fpm; the volume of air being extracted to achieve this flow was 420 cfm.

A modified form of the hood having the same basic construction but designed for use with 5ft ware boards was also found to control the dust efficiently when the velocity over the front opening was not less than 200 fpm for which an extraction volume of 800 cfm was necessary. One domestic earthenware manufacturer has preferred this design of hood to that previously recommended in the First Report for fettling hollow-ware.

Each of the hoods gave satisfactory control of the dust produced during fettling of hand held ware when the majority of the fettled dust is produced. Where 'spotting' and board cleaning is done, the fettling hood selected should enclose the whole of the board during these operations.

When the appropriate fettling hood has been provided it can only effectively control the dust when correctly used. Operators have been seen to fettle hand held ware outside the hood and to do 'spotting' on the open workbench. It is necessary that workers should be fully trained in the correct method of working and they should co-operate fully in discharging their responsibility in safeguarding their own health and that of their fellow workers.

Bone china fettling

The fettling of bone china tableware has also received consideration. The free silica content of this body is normally about 10%–12% and the necessity for achieving the same high standard of dust control as for earthenware, which has a free silica content of about 40%, has been questioned.

Although fettling is a specific source of dust which is capable of easy control, it may no longer be the most serious. With the increased throughput of materials, the 'minor' sources of dust such as floors, benches and general traffic assume much greater importance and may now represent the major problem. Where, however, special steps have been taken to minimise these uncontrolled sources, the general level of atmospheric silica dust may be sufficiently low in bone china manufacture that the need to control the relatively small additions arising from fettling would be less urgent.

Two distinct types of fettling are carried on in bone china manufacturing,

(a) that done by a worker employed as a sponger and fettler, and

(b) that done by the caster himself.

The relatively recent division of labour has followed the pattern of earthenware manufacturing developments except that fettlers are often employed at benches alongside conveyors carrying ware past the fettling points towards the glazing department. Dry fettling occupies a fairly large share of the worker's time and it would be possible for a large proportion of the workers

in any room to be engaged in this process. Where the items being fettled are small there is no practical difficulty in providing hoods of the type described in the First Report, although for larger items it may sometimes be desirable to increase the size of the hood when suitable adjustments should be made to the air flow rates.*

In one particular workroom which had been specially laid out for fettling in this way, and where a very high standard of cleanliness and a good level of general ventilation was maintained, it has been shown that the silica dust concentration in the breathing zone of the fettlers was very low and HM Chief Inspector of Factories is considering whether an exemption from the requirements to provide exhaust ventilation could be granted.

The older method of working is for the caster to fettle his own ware and this is still frequently practised in the case of larger cast items, such as teapots, vegetable dishes and large jugs. Very little time is spent on the dry fettling of these items, sometimes as little as one or two per cent of the total working week, and for this reason the operations have been described as minor fettling. As

* Particulars of dimensions and of air flow rates are available from the Director, British Ceramic Research Association, Queens Road, Penkhull, Stoke-on-Trent, Staffs.

Figure 74: Fettling hood for electro ceramics

the standards of cleanliness in a casting shop cannot at present be maintained at the same level as in a specially designed and constructed fettling department, there is a continuing need to control the dust evolved when fettling although hoods of the type used for earthenware fettling may not be appropriate.

Development work undertaken by the B Ceram. R A has sought to apply the principles of low volume/high velocity dust extraction (Lawrie, 1963, Department of Employment 1970a) to these operations. Earlier difficulties in obtaining sufficiently flexible lightweight tubing have now been overcome and the system is undergoing factory trials. The use of this method of dust control would depend upon HM Chief Inspector of Factories granting exemption from the requirement to carry on the process within a hood.

Secondary dust sources

Secondary dust sources often arise in conjunction with processes which constitute primary dust sources such as the dust released by the handling of ware when towing[3]. The provision of local exhaust ventilation to control these primary dust sources has often controlled, at least in part, the dust arising from secondary sources. When the necessity for local exhaust ventilation is avoided by the elimination of primary dust sources as by substituting wet sponging for dry fettling or towing, there may be need to make separate assessments of secondary dust sources and possibly to apply appropriate control measures.

Recommendations

Efforts to eliminate primary dust sources or reduce them to insignificance should continue but where this is not possible, they should be controlled by efficient exhaust draught. It is recommended that the hoods described in this section and which have been tested and found effective, should be used. Details of air extraction requirements and the minimum air velocity at a given test point found necessary for efficient operation, should be supplied with dust control apparatus. Dust control hoods should incorporate arrangements for collecting the scraps and disposing of them without releasing dust into the air of the workroom.

Efforts to eliminate or reduce secondary dust sources should also be continued. This requires the identification and assessment of such source and the development of remedial measures.

Dust Measuring

The association between the incidence of pneumoconiosis amongst pottery workers and the exposure of the worker to hazardous dust, expressed in terms of duration of exposure and concentration of dust particles in the atmosphere, has long been recognised. In the past there has been difficulty in establishing the nature of this relationship and even in determining dust concentrations. There is also difficulty in establishing the identity of the hazardous constituent, the assumption that the free silica content determines the degree of hazard may be an over simplification but it does give a valuable guide to the extent of the risk. It is generally accepted that the biologically important particles are those within a specified range previously stated as 0.5 to 5 microns projection diameter (Ministry of Labour, 1963). This concept of respirable size is related to the methods of estimating concentrations by counting the number of particles contained in a measured quantity of air. No size selector is needed as the non-respirable particles are separated from the respirable by visual examination.

Instruments used for particulate count determinations consisted essentially of a means of aspirating a measured quantity of air over a dust collecting system so designed that the dust collected could be subsequently examined under a microscope. There were two basic types, the thermal precipitator (Green and Watson, 1935: Watson, 1937) which depended on the phenomenon of the creation of a dust-free zone around a heated wire positioned between two closely spaced microscope slides in such a way that the dust was deposited on the slides, and the impingement device for capturing the dust within an air stream either in a liquid or on a prepared slide.

Figure 75. Penetration curve for the size selector recommended by the Medical Research Council

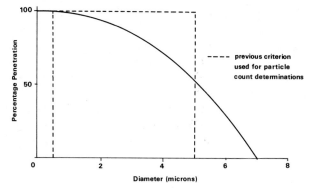

The thermal precipitator has been widely used largely on account of its ability to collect dust in the same form in which it is present in the atmosphere. The basic instrument is designed to operate at 7 ml/min, normally for about half an hour although there are now modified versions available for long period sampling and for collecting dust in the breathing zone by means of a sampling head mounted on a worker's headband. The instrument is battery operated and self-contained.

The instrument on which the work of the American Conference of Government Industrial Hygienists is based is the Greenburg-Smith midget impinger*. In this instrument, air is drawn through a glass jet set a fixed distance from the bottom of a small flask in which is water or alcohol. The particles strike the bottom of the flask and become suspended in the liquid. A sample of the liquid is then placed in a counting cell and the particles counted using a low-power bench microscope. The sampling time is normally about ten minutes or more, if a long sampling time is used, the concentration of dust in the liquid can be diluted by a known factor. Another liquid impinger, the May Three Stage Impinger (May 1966) collects dust in three stages, the airborne dust particles being separated into the three ranges intended to correspond to nasal deposition respiratory system deposition and lower respiratory deposition.

Snatch sampling can be undertaken using a konimeter of which the Zeiss 10 (Roeber, 1957) is a recent introduction. This instrument, like other konimeters, draws a small volume of air through a jet so placed that the dust contained in the air is impacted on a prepared greased glass disc.

The dust spot is subsequently examined under a microscope, in the case of the Zeiss konimeter the microscope is integral. Up to 40 samples can be taken without changing the sample disc. Another sampling instrument, the Draeger Dust Sampler[†], collects dust from 100 cc, or any multiple thereof, of air and separates the dust in a membrane filter which can afterwards be made transparent and the deposit examined under an optical microscope.

Some methods of particulate estimation may have disadvantages including:

(a) the equal emphasis given to dust particles of differing size. It is now generally accepted that the mass of respirable dust in a given volume of air represents a better indication of the health hazard than the number of particles. Past experience demonstrates the difficulty and unreliability of assessing the mass of dust present by counting the number of particles.

*Supplied by Gelman Hawksley, Lancing, Sussex.

Figure 76. B Ceram. R A Gravimpinger

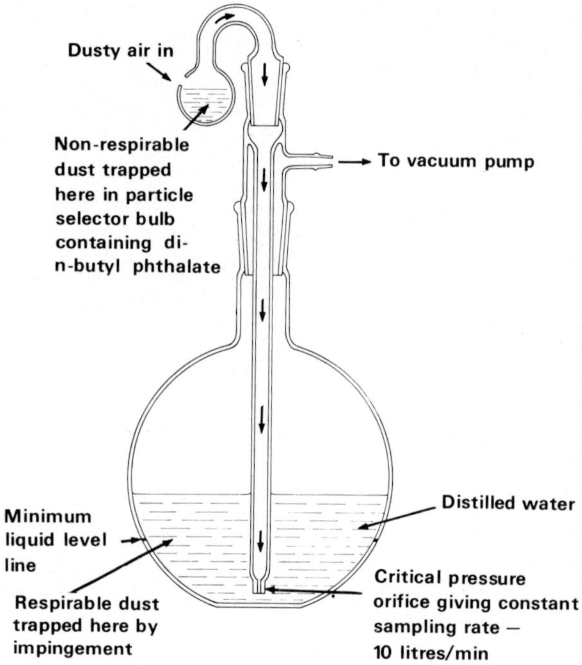

(b) the practical limit inherent in the method of counting dust particles which thereby restricts the volume of air which can be sampled in a given dust concentration. The volume acceptable in a typical pottery situation might be as low as 1cc. Even a series of such a small sample would not give an accurate indication of the dust exposure for a full working week. Long running instruments providing for dilution of the dust collected or for counting only a fraction of the sample partly overcome this difficulty.

(c) the unreliability of the measurements made. Determinations made with different instruments under similar conditions have varied to such an extent that they cannot be used with confidence. This variation could arise, at least in part, from disintegration of aggregates into small particles by the action of the sampling instrument itself.

[†] Supplied by Draeger Normalair Ltd, Kitty Brewster, Blyth, Northumberland.

Figure 77. B Ceram. R A Gravimpinger mounted in a two-deck trolley

(d) the fact that some instruments sample in the general atmosphere of the workroom. This measure may not truly indicate the dust concentration in the air breathed by the worker. The concentration of dust in the breathing zone of a pottery worker is normally significantly greater than that in the general atmosphere of the workroom. A more satisfactory sampling procedure would be to take the air from the breathing zone of the worker as can be done with a modified application of the thermal precipitator.

(e) the inability to differentiate between hazardous and innocuous material. The sample obtained for assessment by counting is adequate for analysis.

Although the particulate count instruments in general are now less favoured for accurate quantitative measurements, they are still useful as a means of identifying dust sources and roughly ranking levels of dust concentration. The konimeter type of instrument is easy to use for this purpose. Some of these defects have been partly overcome by modifications to instruments of which the thermal precipitator appears to have been best adapted, but even this suffers from some of the disadvantages inherent in the method of sampling and assessment. Most of the disadvantages have now been overcome by the development of a new range of instruments with an integral system of size-separation, enabling a sufficiently large sample to be collected for weighing. This enables the dust concentration to be expressed in terms of mass of dust composed of particles within a specified size range per unit volume of air. Recently developed gravimetric instruments are based on a new specification of 'respirable size' (Hamilton and Walton, 1961) in terms of free falling velocity of the particle in air. While this criterion is not based on established biological response, it is related to expected behaviour of the dust particles in the lungs. Size selectors performing to this new specification allow the penetration of a proportion of dust particles of a given size, the proportion varying with size, as indicated in fig. 75.

All of the small particles are permitted to penetrate, but the percentage penetration is reduced as the size increases to give a cut-off at about 7.5 microns. Figure 75 also gives the specification of respirable size as used for visual separation when counting particles.

An acceptable gravimetric instrument should have a size selector meeting this specification followed by a collecting system so designed that a sufficient sample of respirable dust is collected over a large proportion of the working shift or working week to facilitate accurate weighing. Such an instrument operating at a known and constant sampling rate for measured time would give an estimate of the mass of respirable dust in the volume of air drawn through the apparatus. It is further required that there should be means of distinguishing hazardous from non-hazardous dust, possibly by washing out the soluble constituents, ignition of combustible material and accumulating sufficient sample for analysis such as by X-ray diffraction to be carried out.

Particle size separation can be achieved by passing the dust laden air in a slow stream over closely placed horizontal plates so that the non-respirable dust will settle out and this is the method of separation used in the horizontal plate elutriator. Separation of non-respirable dust can also be achieved by changing the direction of the air flow a sufficient number of times to separate out the appropriate fraction of the dust and this is the principle used in the Cascade or May Impinger type separator or in the centrifugal action of a

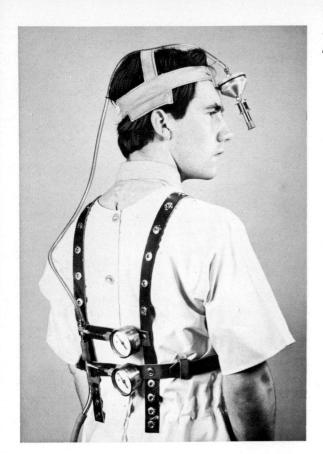

Figure 78. B Ceram. R A
personal dust sampler

mini-cyclone. Another means of separation is by a liquid pre-impinger as fitted to the B Ceram. R A Gravimpinger (Bloor and Dinsdale, 1966). Having separated the non-respirable dust according to the MRC criterion, the instrument must collect and retain the remaining dust in a form suitable for weighing. In practice the dust is normally collected on the filter for direct weighing or in a liquid by impingement from which it can be separated by filtration for subsequent incineration and weighing.

Gravimetric instruments now in use have been developed recently by three research associations under the sponsorship of the Ministry of Technology (Now Department of Trade and Industry). These instruments are fundamentally different as a result of being designed for varying applications and so utilising different principles of size selection and sample collection.

The Gravimpinger (figs 76 and 77) developed by the B Ceram. R A is a mains operated instrument which depends upon a wet pre-impinger for size selection, and a further liquid impinger for dust collection, and is designed for use as a static sampler in the general atmosphere of a workroom over a full working week. The instrument was intended primarily for use by pottery manufacturers. Another gravimetric instrument developed by the B Ceram. R A (Bloor et al 1967) is a sampler utilising a cyclone size selector and a membrane filter mounted on a cap and operated by a mains powered pump. The instrument takes the sample of air from the vicinity of the worker's mouth and nose (fig. 78).

The instrument developed by the British Cast Iron Research Association[*] is also intended to sample near the worker's breathing zone by drawing air through a minicyclone separator and filter collector in a lapel mounted unit. The pump is powered from rechargeable batteries supported in the same harness to make it a self contained apparatus only slightly restricting mobility, fig. 79. The instrument is capable of continuous operation on a single shift of up to eight hours.

[*]Available from C F Casella & Co Ltd London.

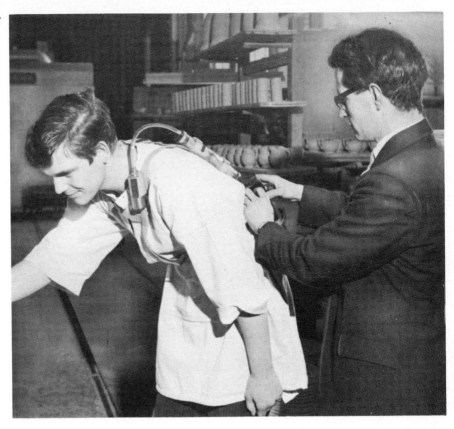

Figure 79. BCIRA personal dust sampler being adjusted for use

Another commercially available instrument is the Hexhlet (Wright 1954) having a built-in power supply to draw air over the horizontal plate elutriator into a filter collector for weighing after incineration. This instrument was developed from work done by the Pneumoconiosis Research Unit of the Medical Research Council.

The majority of dust samplers are intended for survey work by skilled personnel but the B Ceram. R A Gravimpinger was designed as a means of monitoring conditions by individual potteries. It was intended that the sampling method would enable management to assess the effect of measures taken to improve conditions and to guard against subsequent deterioration. A number of Gravimpingers are already in use in the pottery industry for this purpose.

monitor conditions and so indentify those workrooms in which efforts for improvements are most needed or in which conditions have deteriorated. For this purpose a size selecting gravimetric instrument designed for general atmospheric sampling, such as the Gravimpinger, should be used.

Measurements of dust concentrations for the purpose of assessing the hazard to individual workers should be made with a size selecting gravimetric instrument sampling in the breathing zone of the worker.

Recommendations

Regular measurements of atmospheric dust concentrations should be made in all pottery workrooms to

1   Part 3 Tile Manufacturing
2   Appendix 1.3 Engineers Panel
3   Part 2 and Appendix 4.1 Domestic Ware Manufacturing

Proposals
for Progress

Summary of Recommendations for:

The achievement and maintenance of satisfactory conditions in potteries requires the co-operative effort of all, whether directly or indirectly concerned, and whether involved with present methods of production or proposed developments. In the earlier sections of the report, recommendations have been made as to the action which appears to be required; in this section the recommendations are addressed to those who should be concerned with their implementation.

Research and Development

HM Chief Inspector of Factories

Law enforcement

Relaxation of requirements of the Pottery Regulations by means of
exemption should be sympathetically considered where the risk of
pneumoconiosis is significantly reduced by changes in materials or
processes. The use of exemptions to ensure flexibility pending changes in
Regulations should be considered in order to encourage the application of
desirable developments such as floor cleaning machines.

Pneumoconiosis

Support should be given to any scheme of systematic biological
monitoring providing for the initial and periodic medical examination of
workers in the pottery industry exposed to the possible hazard of
pneumoconiosis.

Temperature

The corrected effective temperature scale should be used in preference to
the dry bulb temperature for the purpose of assessing thermal comfort
conditions in potteries.

Medical authorities

Medical Supervision of Workers

Consideration should be given to the establishment of a scheme of
biological monitoring as part of a comprehensive system of medical
supervision of workers in the pottery industry who might be exposed to
dust which could cause pneumoconiosis.

Training Organisations

Suitable general safety courses should be arranged for training persons
appointed to promote safety in potteries.

Operative training should include training in lifting in order to minimise
the risk of sprains and strains when handling materials. Training aids, such
as posters, should be used.

Architects, consulting engineers, heating and ventilation engineers, works engineers etc.

Floors — Construction and drainage

New factories should be so designed and constructed so as to facilitate
the cleaning of floors by daily swilling or wet scrubbing.

Workroom layout

Workroom design and layout should be planned to give the maximum
unrestricted floor area for ease of cleaning.

Temperature

Design criteria

Heating and ventilation systems in potteries should be designed to provide conditions which fall within the corrected effective temperature range of 65 to 71°F (18 − 22°C).

Expert advice

Plans for new or reconstructed potteries should incorporate specialist advice on methods of achieving and maintaining satisfactory temperatures and particular attention should be given to the process which is to be undertaken in the building.

Means of control

Means of controlling the temperature should be provided.

Method of control

Heat emission from plant and kilns should be minimised by insulating to the relevant British Standard with material which is preferably non toxic, of adequate mechanical strength or otherwise protected with a surface which does not readily propagate flame and the surface temperature does not exceed 90°F (32°C) and which permits cleaning. Where appropriate, insulation should be supplemented by the provision of radiant heat shields.

All potteries should be adequately ventilated to ensure the dissipation of heat and provided with means of heating to compensate for excessive heat losses. The outlets of the vent ducts should be so sited as to ensure that hot air cannot return to the workroom.

Siting of kilns

Heated plant, especially kilns, should be so designed, constructed and sited as to minimise the spread of heat and adequate provision incorporated for cooling kiln trucks and ware without the heating being dissipated into the workroom.

Machinery and plant manufacturers and agents

New machines — design of safeguards

New machines should be designed with the minimum of dangerous parts or possibility of dust generation, and where such hazards remain, the machine design should include efficient safeguards.

Provision of safeguards

Machines supplied for use in the pottery industry should be complete with the appropriate safeguards against accident and any necessary enclosure with suitable connections to an air extraction system for the purpose of controlling dust.

Standards of dust control

Manufacturers should specify the design performance of dust control apparatus both in terms of the volume of air to be exhausted and of the air velocity at test positions so that its efficiency may be readily checked.

Precautions against the emission of dust should take account both of primary and secondary sources.

Scrap

New machines should incorporate arrangements for the prevention of spillage and for the interception and collection of scrap for re-processing in such a way that dust is not released into the atmosphere. Where appropriate, local blungers or other effective means should be employed to ensure, as far as possible, that scrap is handled within an enclosed system.

Temperature

All dryers and associated equipment should be so designed that hot air does not escape into the workroom and to this end, feed and delivery openings should be kept as small as possible and an inward flow of air should be maintained whenever the dryer is in operation.

Ventilation ducts at dryers should be sited so that the discharged air cannot re-enter the building and any dampers properly adjusted and secured to prevent the escape of hot air into the workroom. Heated plant should be effectively insulated so that the surface temperature does not exceed 90°F (32°C). Where necessary, the insulation materials should be given adequate mechanical protection or finished to facilitate cleaning, but no protective finish should be used which readily propagates flame. Non toxic materials should be used wherever possible.

Kilns and similarly heated plant should be so designed, constructed and sited as to minimise the likelihood of heat spread into other parts of the premises.

Existing machines

Where improved standards of safety and dust control are devised for new machines, wherever possible modifications should be made available to existing machine users.

Pottery Manufacturers

New machinery and plant

Orders for new plant and machines should specifically require the recommendations addressed to machinery manufacturers to be observed and when appropriate, machine makers should be expected to have satisfied HM Factory Inspectorate as to the adequacy of safeguards against mechanical hazards and dust.

Before being brought into use, checks should be made to ensure that all necessary safeguards are properly fitted and that when tested, dust control apparatus performs to the specified standard.

New and reconstructed buildings

New buildings should be constructed to comply with the recommendations addressed to architects.

Safety — standards of safeguards

The higher standards of safeguards made possible by developments in safety techniques should be applied wherever practicable to existing machines and plant.

A system of regular inspection by a competent person should be instituted to ensure that safeguards provided at gas fired plant are properly maintained.

Safety in handling

Manual handling should be so arranged as to minimise the risk of sprains and strains and wherever possible mechanical assistance should be provided.

Appropriate protection for the fingers and hands should be made available for use when the work makes it desirable.

Safety supervision

In each pottery a person of sufficient seniority should be specifically appointed to promote safety generally and to investigate accidents with a view to eliminating the hazards which give rise to them.

Temperature — levels of controls

The corrected effective temperature of pottery workrooms should be within the range $65°F - 71°F$ ($18°C - 22°C$) and satisfactory means of control should be provided, including adequate ventilation to dissipate excess heat and means of heating to compensate for excessive heat losses.

Insulation

All dryers and associated equipment should be maintained so that hot air does not escape into the workroom and to this end, feed and delivery openings should be kept as small as possible and an inward flow of air should be maintained whenever the dryer is in operation.

Ventilation ducts at dryers should be sited so that the discharged air cannot re-enter the building and any dampers properly adjusted and secured to prevent the escape of hot air into the workroom.

Heated plant should be insulated so that the surface temperature does not exceed $90°F$ ($32°C$). Where necessary the insulation materials should be given adequate mechanical protection or finished to facilitate cleaning, but no protective finish should be used which readily propagates flame. Non toxic materials should be used wherever possible.

Kilns and similarly heated plant should be sited to minimise the likelihood of heat spread into other parts of the premises.

Scrap

Pottery manufacturing should be so arranged by management as to minimise the spillage of materials on floors, especially in gangways or working aisles. Existing machines and processes should be examined and modified wherever practicable to eliminate or reduce the production of scrap and to ensure that such scraps as are unavoidably generated are efficiently contained, collected and re-processed with the minimum of release of dust or material. To this end a comprehensive and integrated system should be provided wherever possible based on a local blunger for conversion of the scrap into a slip for piped return to the body processing department. Where local slip conversion is not practicable, purpose-designed containers should be provided for collection and conveyance and such containers should be emptied directly into the scrap blunger. Where loading into the blunger is mechanised, the opportunity should be taken to provide local exhaust ventilation. Improved bins, such as the swing lid type, should be used for the scrap resulting from hand operations.

Dust control

Efforts to identify and eliminate all sources of atmospheric dust and to eliminate or reduce them to insignificance should continue and where this is not possible they should be controlled by efficient exhaust draught. Dust control hoods should incorporate arrangements for collecting the scraps and disposing of them without releasing dust into the air of the workroom.

Efforts to eliminate or reduce secondary dust sources should also continue. This requires the identification and assessment of such sources and the development of remedial measures

Floor cleaning

Methods of cleaning floors should be such as to remove thoroughly the material which would otherwise give rise to dust without themselves contributing significantly to the atmospheric dust concentration. Wherever practicable cleaning should be by swilling or wet scrubbing by machine.

Cleaning should be completed as soon as possible after the material is spilled on the floor and in any case not later than the interval at the end of the shift.

Workroom layout and plant arrangements should be planned to provide the maximum unrestricted floor area for ease and efficiency of cleaning.

Dust measurements

Regular measurements of atmospheric dust concentrations should be made in all pottery workrooms to monitor conditions and so identify those workrooms in which improvements are most needed or in which conditions have deteriorated. For this purpose a size selecting gravimetric instrument designed for general atmospheric sampling, such as the Gravimpinger, should be used.

Sectional

Flint processing

Wherever possible all crushing, grinding and conveying should be carried out within a closed circuit with adequate air extraction to prevent the escape of dust from the plant. Until this ideal is achieved high standards of dust control should be provided at all points where dust might otherwise be evolved. Effective monitoring should be undertaken to ensure that standards of dust control are properly maintained.

Tile manufacturing

Efforts to reduce the silica content of tile body should continue. Special care should be exercised to ensure that mechanisation and other process changes do not increase dust evolution, but rather changes should be exploited to prevent dust emissions. Continuing attention should be paid to secondary dust control, particularly spillage, floor cleaning and handling, and the aim should be to achieve, as far as possible, production entirely within a closed circuit system.

Sanitary whiteware manufacturing

Sanitary whiteware manufacturers should examine their methods of production with special regards to (a) the need to eliminate the spillage of materials on floors, (b) the need to provide local exhaust ventilation for all fettling operations giving rise to dust and (c) the need to clean workbenches as required by the Pottery Regulations. Dilution ventilation should be recognised as a secondary safeguard, its principles clarified and correctly implemented. Good general ventilation is invariably necessary. With regard to future developments, health should be of major concern in any change of (a) materials where free silica reduction should be the primary aim, and (b) methods, where the aim should be to avoid the introduction of any new process and plant which results directly or indirectly in the pollution of the air of the workroom.

Domestic ware manufacturing

Any change in body composition should be such as to reduce the respirable free silica content. Means should be sought to eliminate the use of free silica in subsidiary processes such as case making with resins or in the placing of earthenware for biscuit firing. As far as possible the aim should be to achieve production within an enclosed system.

Ground stone supplied for bone china manufacturing should be transported, delivered and used in slop form.

British Pottery Manufacturers' Federation

To ensure the uniform attainment of high standards of safety and health and to avoid unnecessary duplication of effort, machinery should be established for the sharing of ideas at a practical level, possibly the undertaking of joint development in appropriate projects and the establishment of means of propagating information and advice peculiar to the pottery industry

Operatives

Appendix 1

1.1 Potters' Shops Sub-Committee at 1967

G P Brown (*Chairman*), W A Bloor (*Co-opted from the B Ceram. RA*), J M W Davis, A Dinsdale, A Dulson, J M Palmer (*Co-opted from the B Ceram. RA*), D P Shelley, L R Sillitoe, D J Evans (*Secretary*)

Previous Members: N Fish, S Hobson, V B Jones, Miss L A Pittom, P H Royle, N Wilson

1.2 Technical Sub-Committee (From November 1967)

J D G Hammer (*Chairman*), W A Bloor (*Co-opted from B Ceram. RA*), J M W Davis, A Dinsdale, J M Palmer (*Co-opted from B Ceram. RA*), L R Sillitoe, N Walters, N L Wright, D J Evans (*Secretary*)

1.3 Members of the Panel of Engineers

G W Bird, F Inst Ceram AMIW, *Chief Engineer Johnson Bros*
G P Brown C Eng AMI Mech E, *HM District Inspector of Factories (Chairman)*
H Calderbank C Eng AMI Mech EAMI Loco E, *HM Inspector of Factories*
J M Palmer C Eng AMI Mech E, *Senior Experimental Officer B Ceram. RA*
J W Rieveley B Sc Tech C Eng AMI Mech E, *Chief Engineer Alfred Meakin (Tunstall) Limited*
J Robinson B Sc C Eng AMI Mech E ACGI, *Chief Engineer Josiah Wedgwood & Sons Ltd*

Appendix 2

Pneumoconiosis Compensation Schemes

From 1906 to 1946, successive Workmen's Compensation Acts empowered the Secretary of State to make schemes for the payment of compensation by the employers of workmen at risk through exposure to silica dust in specified industries and processes. The first scheme providing compensation for pottery workers was made in 1928 but was restricted to those cases where death or total disablement resulted or where there was disablement accompanied by tuberculosis. The scheme of 1931, which replaced this first provision, included the important change that partial disablement was included and routine initial and periodic medical examinations were prescribed in scheduled occupations. The scheme made under these Acts required that a man found to be suffering from silicosis should automatically be suspended from the work which caused the disease and the compensation designed as recompense for the loss of earnings which necessarily follow.

The National Insurance (Industrial Injuries) Act 1946 which came into operation in July 1948 superseded the old Workmen's Compensation Act; Instead of compensation for loss of earnings, disablement benefit is paid on assessment of loss of faculty expressed as a percentage representing the extent to which the worker is handicapped by the disease and thereby prevented from carrying on the ordinary activities of life as compared with a normal healthy person of the same age. When the disablement necessitated a change or cessation of work an additional allowance could be made.

A further scheme, the Pneumoconiosis and Byssinosis Benefit Scheme, which came into operation in 1952 was designed to provide cover for a limited range of workers who were disabled by pneumoconiosis but who were unable to qualify for benefit under the Industrial Injuries Act because the causative employment ended before the Act came into operation in July 1948, and who were time-barred from claiming under the Workmens Compensation Acts. Initially, this scheme also applied only where disablement was total, but from 1954, benefit was extended to the partially disabled, the payment made still being intended as compensation for loss of earnings.

The Silicosis Medical Board under the old Workmen's Compensation Act were staffed by the same doctors as the Pneumoconiosis Medical Panel administered by the Ministry of Pensions and National Insurance, now the Department of Health and Social Security, under the National Insurance (Industrial Injuries) Act. The Pneumoconiosis and Byssinosis Benefit Scheme is administered by a separate Board but the same doctors as in the other schemes are responsible for medical certification. Thus the first assessments reported by the Pneumoconiosis Medical Panels include all cases of benefit under any of the three schemes.

New applicants for compensation under the Workmen's Compensation Acts have now ceased, although compensation continues to be paid in some instances. All applicants for pension are now dealt with under the National Insurance (Industrial Injuries) Act or the Pneumoconiosis and Byssinosis Benefit Scheme.

Awards of benefit may arise from application following diagnosis through the National Health Service or by means of the scheme of compulsory initial and periodic examinations of workpeople employed in certain specified occupations. This system of regular and medical examinations continued that which had earlier applied under the Workmen's Compensation Schemes, but the new Act coming into force in 1948, following the disruption of the war years prevented the scheme from becoming fully operational until 1954.

Appendix 3

3.1 Assessments for pneumoconiosis pensions attributable to the North Staffs and all GB pottery industry 1950-1969

Year	North Staffordshire			All GB		Deaths
	Number	3 years moving average	3 year totals	Number	3 year totals	
	a	b	c	d	e	f
1950	52			128		73
1951	48	55	165	135	416	62
1952	65	114		153		70
1953	229	167		354		79
1954	206	233	698	345	1081	62
1955	263	255		382		76
1956	295	235		432		104
1957	146	210	630	233	924	91
1958	189	129		259		84
1959	52	92		89		83
1960	34	46	139	50	207	90
1961	53	51		68		101
1962	65	60		99		70
1963	63	57	172	76	240	72
1964	44	50		65		79
1965	43	35		62		68
1966	19	26	79	27	120	65
1967	17	21		31		46
1968	27	20		30		56
1969	17			28		39

Source:

a Stoke-on-Trent Pneumoconiosis Medical Panel.

d Annual Reports of the Department of Health and Social Security, 1950-1969.

f Annual Reports of HM Chief Inspector of Factories 1950-1969.

3.2   New assessments for pneumoconiosis pensions attributable to the North Staffs pottery industry 1953-4 and 1965-9

(a)   Distribution by disability

Years	Assessed Disability %											
	≤10	20	30	40	50	60	70	80	90	100	Totals	Average[2]
1953	81	71	31	11	9	5	4	1	1	15	229	17.4
1954[1]	102	53	21	5	4		2	2		17	206	13.3
Total	183	124	52	16	13	5	6	3	1	32	435	
%	43	29	12	4	4	1	2	1	<.2	8	100	15.5
1965	35	2	4	2							43	8.7
1966*	8	5	3		1					2	19	12.7
1967	15	2									17	6.2
1968	24	1	2								27	6.1
1969*	14	2								1	17	6.4
Total	96	12	9	2	1					3	123	
%	79	10	7	2	1					3	100	

Source: Stoke-on-Trent Pneumoconiosis Medical Panel

[1] Includes 1 posthumous award   *Includes 2 posthumous awards
[2] 100% disability cases excluded as an unknown proportion of the disability is attributable to pneumoconiosis and all ≤10% counted as 5% for calculating the average.

3.2   (b)   Distribution by duration of exposure

Years	Years exposure												
	≤14	15-19	20-24	25-29	30-34	35-39	40-44	45-49	50-54	55-59	60 & over	Total	Average[1]
1953	9	11	16	32	40	49	33	20	10	7	2	229	35.3
1954	2	7	14	24	35	48	35	22	14	4	1	206	37.0
Total	11	18	30	56	75	97	68	42	24	11	3	435	
%	3	4	7	13	17	22	15	10	5	3	1	100	36.1
1965	1	3	9	9	4	3	6	8				43	34.2
1966	2		2	6		1	3	4			1	19	34.3
1967	1	1	3	3	3	1	2	1	2			17	30.7
1968	1	4	4	2	7	2	3	3	1			27	31.6
1969		1	3	2	3	2	4	1	1			17	34.3
Total	5	9	21	22	17	9	18	17	4		1	123	
%	4	7	17	17	14	9	15	14	3		1	100	34.2

Source: Stoke-on-Trent Pneumoconiosis Medical Panel

[1] In calculating the average ≤14 have been counted 10-14 and 60 and over as 60-65.

3.2 (c) Distribution by age

Years	25-29	30-34	35-39	40-44	45-49	50-54	55-59	60-64	65-69	70-74	75-80	80	Total	Average
1953		7	8	25	38	53	31	39	21	6	1		229	53.8
1954			4	19	25	49	38	38	24	6	2	1	206	55.2
Total		7	12	44	63	102	69	77	45	12	3	1	435	
%		2	3	10	14	23	14	15	10	3	1	.5	100	54.5
1965			1	4	6	8	11	9	3	1			43	52.8
1966				1	4	3	4	4	1	1		1	19	57.5
1967				2	2	3	6	2	1	1			17	55.7
1968				3	4	2	10	5	2	1			27	54.9
1969				3	4	2	3	3		1	1		17	54.9
Total			1	13	20	18	34	23	7	5	1	1	123	
%			1	11	17	15	29	19	6	4	1	1	100	54.2

Source: Stoke-on-Trent Pneumoconiosis Medical Panel.

3.3 Reported accidents in North Staffs and all GB potteries 1957-1969

Year	North Staffs Potteries			GB Potteries			
	Reported Accidents	Workers 1,000	Incidence Rate Accidents per 1,000	All[1] Reported Accidents	Reported[2] Accidents in Pottery Processes	Workers[3] 1,000	Incidence[4] Rate Accidents per 1,000
	a	b	c	d	e	f	g
1957				920			
1958				910			
1959				1,116	1,055	58.9	17.9
1960				1,093	1,063	57.6	18.5
1961				1,066	1,021	58.4	17.5
1962	719	42.4	17.0	958	910	59.4	15.3
1963	739	40.9	18.1	1,070	1,000	55.5	18.0
1964	1,074	40.2	26.7	1,560	1,460	56.8	25.7
1965	1,099	39.5	27.8	1,544	1,500	56.0	26.8
1966	1,073	33.8	27.7	1,543	1,459	56.5	25.8
1967	988	38.0	26.0	1,418	1,374	54.0	25.4
1968	1,042	38.2	27.3	1,529	1,515	51.3	29.5
1969	1,247	38.3	32.6	1,777	1,752	51.9	33.8

Source:
a   JSC records.
b   Census of Employment.
d-g   HM Chief Inspector of Factories Annual Reports. 1962-69.

Note [1]   Totals include all reported accidents in factories in which pottery manufacture is the principal occupation.
[2]   Excludes those accidents in column d which do not arise from pottery processes.
[3]   Estimated number of workers subject to the Factories Act — Establishments where pottery manufacture is the principal occupation.
[4]   This incidence rate may not be directly comparable with North Staffs column c, because of the factors noted 1-3 and so should be used primarily to indicate a trend over the period 1959-69.

3.4 Reported accidents in the North Staffs pottery industry — Distribution by cause

	1957*	1958*	1959*	1960*	1961*	1962	1963	1964	1965	1966	1967	1968	1969	Total 1967-69	% 1967-69
Handling	371	341	373	403	396	251	255	361	369	399	343	316	420	1079	31
Persons falling	169	184	227	189	181	117	134	188	196	193	166	190	194	550	17
Transport															
Rail	2	1	9	25	22	25	22	27	38	41	35	45	59	139	4
Non-rail	29	21	65	64	70	63	64	83	93	113	86	110	113	309	9
Striking against objects	84	91	93	98	92	89	86	154	135	134	138	90	113	341	11
Machinery power and non-power	57	64	101	113	110	72	79	114	106	71	71	80	89	240	7
Struck by falling object	61	47	46	48	52	41	44	70	97	44	63	62	82	207	6
Hand tools	28	29	33	37	40	23	27	42	24	30	33	34	28	95	3
Other	92	90	92	67	61	38	28	35	41	48	53	115	154	322	10
Totals	893	868	1039	1044	1024	719	739	1074	1099	1073	988	1042	1252	3282	100

Source: HM Factory Inspectorate, Stoke-on-Trent

* Includes all GB reported pottery accidents

3.5 Reported accidents in all GB factory processes — Distribution by cause

Thousands

	1959	1960	1961	1962	1963	1964	1965	1966	1967	1968	1969	Total 1967-69	% 1967-69
Handling	38.88	42.07	42.15	40.13	42.80	58.84	69.15	64.59	67.37	69.00	72.44	208.81	27
Persons falling	22.38	24.58	24.34	24.79	26.59	31.05	34.45	35.45	36.70	37.28	38.85	112.83	15
Transport													
Rail	1.20	1.10	1.03	0.96	1.09	1.26	1.33	1.09	1.11	1.10	1.10	3.31	.5
Non-Rail	8.96	9.77	9.83	10.06	11.36	15.64	17.66	17.81	18.44	19.83	20.64	58.91	8
Striking against object	11.43	12.75	13.12	12.76	13.57	18.08	20.85	23.13	22.97	22.98	23.26	69.21	9
Machinery Power & Non-power	28.53	31.17	31.79	30.92	32.98	42.89	45.47	43.94	42.87	44.65	46.16	133.68	18
Struck by falling object	11.80	13.30	13.16	12.62	12.59	16.38	14.49	18.91	17.58	18.19	19.23	55.00	7
Hand tools	11.80	12.17	12.07	11.29	12.06	15.30	16.07	15.88	16.70	17.69	18.27	52.66	7
Other	13.52	14.61	14.17	14.08	15.07	18.51	19.69	20.25	21.82	23.74	26.91	72.47	9
Total	148.50	161.52	161.66	157.61	168.11	217.95	239.16	241.05	245.56	254.46	266.86	766.88	100

Source: Annual Reports HM Chief Inspector of Factories 1957-69.

3.6   Reported accidents in North Staffs potteries and all GB factory processes — Distribution by nature of injury

| Nature of Injury | North Staffordshire Potteries | | | | | All GB Factory[1] Processes 1968 | |
	1967	Number 1968	1969	Total 1967-69	% 1967-69	Thousands	%
Cuts and abrasions etc.	431	412	568	1411	43	117.69[2]	46
Sprains and strains	371	376	444	1191	35	65.05	25
Fractures and dislocations	116	141	130	387	12	27.36	11
Eye injuries	2	9	10	21	1	9.60	4
Burns and scalds	16	12	21	49	2	9.11	4
Multiple injuries	5	8	3	16	1	5.35	2
Amputations	7	11	9	27	1	2.96	1
Others	40	73	62	175	5	17.34	7
Totals	988	1042	1247	3277	100	254.45	100

Source:
North Staffs: HM Factory Inspectorate, Stoke-on-Trent
All UK: HM Chief Inspector of Factories

Note: [1] Analysis of all GB factory processes accidents according to nature of injury is completed on a 3 year cycle; the last available figures shown do not vary significantly from the previous distribution given for 1965 in the Chief Inspector of Factories Annual Report.

[2] 'Cuts and Abrasions' include:

crushing	4122
open wounds	53808
bruising and surface injury	59761
total	117691

3.7   Reported accidents in North Staffs potteries and all GB factory processes — Distribution by site of injury

| Site of Injury | North Staffordshire Potteries | | | | | All GB Factory[1] Processes 1968 | |
	1967	Number 1968	1969	Total 1967-69	% 1967-69	Thousands	%
Head	34	54	58	146	5	19.73	8
Trunk	317	307	389	1013	31	60.29	24
Hands and arms	329	317	357	1003	31	91.63	36
Feet and legs	267	312	367	946	28	72.22	28
Multiple site						4.99	2
Others, irrespective of site (eg sepsis, shock, poisoning, suffocation)	41	52	76	169	5	5.59	2
Totals	988	1042	1247	3277	100	254.45	100

Sources:
North Staffs: HM Factory Inspectorate, Stoke-on-Trent
All UK: HM Chief Inspector of Factories

Note: [1] Analysis of all GB Factory processes accidents according to site of injury is completed on a 3 year cycle; the last available figures shown do not vary significantly from the previous distribution given for 1965 in the Chief Inspector of Factories Annual Report.

.8　Reported machinery accidents — North Staffs pottery industry — Distribution by machine

	1957*	1958*	1959*	1960*	1961*	1962	1963	1964	1965	1966	1967	1968	1969	Total 1957-61	Total 1965-69	Total 1957-69
Pug mill	—	1	3	3	6	2	4	2	1	2	—	2	2	13	7	28
Pan mill	3	3	—	5	3	2	3	3	3	—	1	3	5	14	12	34
Semi automatic making machines																
flat	7	5	4	15	9	6	2	10	13	7	6	2	5	40	33	91
cup	6	12	14	11	10	7	10	19	16	10	5	9	4	53	44	133
Roller making machines	—	—	—	—	—	—	1	1	2	—	2	2	1	—	7	9
Presses hand	3	2	7	7	9	4	4	10	3	3	—	3	—	28	9	55
Semi automatic	3	4	5	—	4	5	4	—	4	3	1	2	1	16	11	36
automatic	2	2	4	4	—	1	1	3	6	1	2	4	4	12	17	34
other	—	—	4	6	7	4	3	3	5	1	7	6	12	17	31	58
Semi automatic towing	—	—	—	—	—	—	—	—	—	—	3	3	1	—	7	7
Turning machines	—	—	4	3	3	1	1	2	4	—	3	—	5	10	12	26
Tile dipping	—	1	3	—	6	2	2	1	—	1	1	2	2	10	6	21
Murray Curvex printing	4	—	5	3	—	1	3	1	1	2	2	1	1	12	7	24
Grinding	1	3	8	3	5	4	4	3	1	—	8	3	3	20	15	46
Sorting	3	1	1	4	1	1	2	2	2	—	2	2	—	10	6	21
Lifting machinery	—	4	4	1	1	5	3	5	4	2	4	4	6	10	20	43
Conveyor machinery	7	1	2	2	2	1	7	6	8	8	10	9	11	14	46	74
Others	18	25	33	46	44	26	25	33	33	31	14	23	26	166	127	377
Total	57	64	101	113	110	72	79	104	106	71	71	80	89	445	417	1117

Source: HM Factory Inspectorate, Stoke-on-Trent

*Includes reported accident in all GB potteries

Appendix 4

4.1 Semi-Automatic Towing Machine
(See illustration overleaf)

Manufacturers: Service (Engineers) Ltd, Stoke-on-Trent

Dry finishing of flat clay ware can be undertaken by this machine which smooths both the face and the edges with abrasive pads. The ware is placed by hand on one of the four whirlers on which the ware is mechanically centred and rotated between the pads as the machine table indexes round, so enabling the operator to remove the smooth ware and to replace it by another piece at the feed position.

The smoothing operation, like the towing which it replaced, produces much dust for which purpose enclosure with exhaust ventilation is provided. Secondary dust was found to rise from the handling of ware at the machine, especially at the ware loading and off-loading tables. The provision of back plates at these tables directs the inward air flow at the hood across the table so giving control of this secondary dust.

The JSC for the pottery industry accepted the dust control apparatus which had been tested by the B Ceram. RA and found satisfactory to control the dust produced at the Service semi-automatic towing machine. This recognition was subject to the appliance being properly installed, operated and maintained and was without prejudice to any further developments or improvements.

SPECIFICATIONS

Construction
The hood should be constructed to Service (Engineers) drawing DSEL 767 and the front opening partially blanked off by a flexible plastic curtain to reduce the height of the opening to about four inches.

Air Extraction
A minimum air extraction rate of 650 cfm is required which should give an air flow of not less than 100 fpm at a test position 6 inches above the centre of each ware platform.

Availability
As dry finishing has now been superseded by wet sponging, this machine is less commonly used. Although later models were supplied with the improved method of dust control some of the earlier machines may require modification by the manufacturers.

4.2 Vibro Energy Mill

Manufacturers: William Boulton Ltd, Stoke-on-Trent

In the past, adhering sand and placing material has been removed from biscuit ware by brushing. This hand operation can now be accomplished in the vibro energy mill which is basically a circular vibrating trough filled with hard wood chips. In operation the ware passes round the trough due to the vibratory motion and is separated from the chips as it passes over a raised grid to the unloading position. Except for an area at the front where the operatives work, the trough is covered by a tough plastic sheet.

The cleaning process gives rise to dust for which reason dust control apparatus is provided by the manufacturers as an integral part of the machine. There is partial enclosure at the loading and unloading points to ensure that air flows past the operator into the machine through the front opening over the trough. Air is extracted downwards from the trough and from the enclosed space above the vibrating chips and ware.

Two machines of different sizes were tested by the B Ceram. RA which found that the extraction system effectively controlled the dust when the following conditions were satisfied:

	Model FM 10	Model FM 40
Drawing No	52/58	58/39/A
Air Extraction above trough	500 cfm	650 cfm
below trough		600 cfm
Vertical air velocity loading area	265 fpm	250 fpm
unloading area	155 fpm	

Appendix 5

References

Bedford T (1940) Environmental Warmth and its Measurement. In Medical Research Council War Memorandum 17, HMSO London.

Birmingham Regional Hospital Board (1953-1970). Annual Report of the Miniature Mass Radiography Service, Stoke-on-Trent. 1952-1969.

Bloor W A & Dinsdale A (1966). Annals of Occupation Hygiene, 9, 29.

Bloor W A, Eardley R E and Dinsdale A (1967) British Ceramic Research Association Research Paper 604.

British Standards Institute (1963). The use of Thermal Insulating Materials in the temperature range 200°F — 450°F (95°C — 230°C) CP 1528 (63). The Council for Codes of Practice, British Standards Institute, London.

British Standards Institute (1964). The use of Thermal Insulating Materials between 450°F and 1200°F (230°C to 650°C) CP 3708 (64). The Council for Codes of Practice, British Standards Institute, London.

City of Stoke-on-Trent (1958-1969). Youth Employment Service, Annual Reports 1958-1969. Stoke-on-Trent.

Department of Employment (1952-1970) Annual Reports of HM Chief Inspector of Factories 1951-1969 HMSO London.

Department of Employment (1969) Accidents No 79. How they are caused and how to prevent them. HMSO London.

Department of Employment (1970a) Threshold Limit Values for 1969. Technical Data Note 2/70, HMSO London.

Department of Employment (1970b) Dust Control in the low-volume/high-velocity system. Technical Data Note 1 HMSO London.

Department of Health and Social Security (1944-1949) (Previously Ministry of Pensions and National Insurance) Report 1944-1949 HMSO London

Department of Health and Social Security (1950-1969) Annual Reports 1950-1969 HMSO London

Evans D J (1969) Methods and Processes of the Future. Ceramics, Vol 20 No 244

Evans & Finnikin. (in preparation) Methods of cleaning pottery floors and means of assessing their effectiveness.

Evans & Posner (1971) Pneumoconiosis in Laundry Workers. Environmental Research, 4.121 New York.

Gilson, J C (1969) The Changing Pattern of Pneumoconiosis. In 'Health Conditions in the Ceramic Industry' Ed C N Davies, Pergamon Press, Oxford.

Gloyne, S Roodhouse (1951) Pneumoconiosis, a Histological Survey of Necropsy materials in 1205 cases. Lancet 1.

Green H L & Watson H H (1935) Physical Methods for the estimation of the dust hazard in industry. Medical Research Council Special Report Series 199, HMSO London.

Gregory L & Smyth R L (in prep). The Worker and the Pottery Industry; Department of Economic Studies on the British Pottery Industry No 4 Keele University.

Fox R H (1965) Ergonomics for Industry: Thermal Comfort in Industry HMSO London.

Hamilton R J and Walton W H (1961) In Inhaled Particles and Vapours Ed C N Davies, Pergamon Press, Oxford.

Hunter D (1955) Diseases of Occupation, EUP London.

Institute of Heating and Ventilating Engineers (1965) IHVE Guide, 3rd edition. London.

International Labour Office (1959) Occupational Health and Safety, 9, 2.

Joint Standing Committee for the Pottery Industry
(1960) Safety in the operation of Pottery Kilns and Ovens. National Joint Council, Stoke-on-Trent.
(1967A) Use of Hydrofluoric Acid. Private memorandum of manufacturers. HM Factory Inspectorate, Stoke-on-Trent.
(1967b) Environmental Temperature Control in Potteries. Private memorandum to all manufacturers, HM Factory Inspectorate, Stoke-on-Trent.
(1967c) Terylene Protective Clothing for Pottery Workers. Private memorandum to all manufacturers, HM Factory Inspectorate, Stoke-on-Trent.
(1968a) Dust Control Arrangements for the hand fettling of electrical Porcelain Dust Pressed Ware. Private memorandum to electro-ceramic manufacturers, HM Factory Inspectorate, Stoke-on-Trent.
(1968b) Mould Making. Private memorandum to manufacturers, HM

Factory Inspectorate, Stoke-on-Trent.
(1969a) Scrap Containment, collection and disposal. Private memorandum to large manufacturers, HM Factory Inspectorate, Stoke-on-Trent.
(1969b) Use of Oil in Pottery Manufacture. Private memorandum to manufacturers, HM Factory Inspectorate, Stoke-on-Trent.
(1970a) The provision of protection for fingers and hands. Private memorandum to manufacturers. HM Factory Inspectorate, Stoke-on-Trent.
(1970b) Use of Stone in Bone China Manufacture. Private memorandum to manufacturers. HM Factory Inspectorate, Stoke-on-Trent.

Lawrie W B (1963) The Control of Dust at Source. Paper published at 3rd World Congress on the Prevention of Industrial Hazards, Paris 1963.

May K R (1966) Multistage Liquid Impinger. Bacteriological Reviews, 1966 Vol 30. No 3.

Meiklejohn A (1969) The History of Respiratory Disease in the North Staffs Pottery Industry. In health Conditions in the Ceramic Industry Ed. C N Davies, Pergamon Press, Oxford.

Ministry of Labour (1963) Dust Control in Potteries First Report of the Joint Standing Committee for the Pottery Industry, HMSO London

Ministry of Labour & National Service (1943) Report of a Committee Appointed to Consider Methods of Suppression and Removal of Dust Containing Silica in the Tile Making and the Electrical Porcelain Fittings sections of the Pottery Industry, HMSO London.

Ministry of Labour & National Service (1959) Industrial Health — A Survey of the Pottery Industry in Stoke-on-Trent, HMSO London.

Machin D J & Smyth R L (1970) The British Pottery Industry 1935-1968 Department of Economic Studies on the British Pottery Industry No 2 Keele University.

Ministry of Power (1955) Annual Digest of Pneumoconiosis Statistics 1955, HMSO London.

Ministry of Technology (1970) The Report of the Enquiry into Safety of Natural Gas as Fuel. HMSO London.

National Council of the Pottery Industry (1933) Floors of Potters' Shops Interim Report of the Research, Inventions and Designs Committee. Stoke-on-Trent.

Appendix 6

Acknowledgments

National Board for Prices and Incomes (1970) Pay and other terms of employment of workers in the pottery industry. Report No 149 HMSO London.

Posner E (1957) British Journal of Tuberculosis and Disease of the Chest.

Posner E (1969) Pneumoconiosis in the North Staffs Pottery Industry. In 'Health Conditions in the Ceramic Industry' Ed C N Davies Pergamon Press, Oxford.

Posner E and Kennedy MCS (1967) A Further Study of China Biscuit Placers In Stoke-on-Trent, British Journal of Industrial Medicine 24, 133.

Roeber R (1957) Untersuchungen zur konimetrischen staubmessung. I Staub 1957 No 48.

Statutory Instrument No 65 (1950) Pottery (Health & Welfare) Special Regulations 1950, HMSO London.

Statutory Rules and Orders (1913) Regulations for the Manufacture and Decoration of Pottery, SR & O No 2, 1913. HMSO London.

Statutory Rules and Orders (1932) The Pottery (Silicosis) Regulations SR & O 393, 1932, HMSO London.

Social and Economic Research Interdepartmental Committee (1969) Report on the Census of Production 1963. HMSO London.

Wainwright D & Evans D J (1969) Orthopaedic Conditions and Accidents in the Pottery Industry. In 'Health Conditions in the Ceramic Industry' Ed C N Davies, Pergamon Press, Oxford.

Watson H H (1937) A system for obtaining from Mines Air dust samples for physical, chemical and petrological examination. Trans. Institution of Mining and Metallurgy, Vol XLVI, 1936-7.

Weiland W (1970) Experience with Communal Body Preparations. In "Interceram" Vol 19, No 1.

Wright B M (1954) British Journal of Industrial Medic. 11, 284.

This report is the result of the efforts of numerous individuals and organisations over a long period, and their help and co-operation is gratefully acknowledged even where they cannot now be named. In particular the Joint Standing Committee wish to express its thanks to

The British Ceramic Research Association and its Director, Dr N Astbury.

The Principal and staff of the North Staffordshire Polytechnic (previously the North Staffordshire College of Technology), where the Department of Ceramics under Dr German has continued its valuable work in training Works Inspectors and disseminating information and advice to the many students from the pottery industry.

The Stoke-on-Trent Pneumoconiosis Medical Panel and its Senior Member, Dr Coles, who continued to co-operate closely with HM Factory Inspectorate and provided much of the data on which Part 2 of this report is based.

The Miniature Mass Radiography Unit, Stoke-on-Trent and its Director, Dr E Posner, Consultant Chest Physician.

The Panel of Engineers whose report on Environmental Temperature Control in Potteries formed the basis of Temperature Control in Part 4 of this report, and their respective employers who granted time and facilities for undertaking the study.

The many pottery manufacturers who co-operated in carrying out experiments and development work at considerable expense and inconvenience.

The constant assistance and support of HM Chief Inspector of Factories.

The Director of the Industrial Hygiene Section and the staff of the Chemical Branch of HM Factory Inspectorate.